SOUL
TATTOO

SOUL
TATTOO

A LIFE AND SPIRIT BEARING
THE MARKS OF GOD

SAMUEL KEE

transforming lives together

SOUL TATTOO
Published by David C Cook
4050 Lee Vance View
Colorado Springs, CO 80918 U.S.A.

David C Cook Distribution Canada
55 Woodslee Avenue, Paris, Ontario, Canada N3L 3E5

David C Cook U.K., Kingsway Communications
Eastbourne, East Sussex BN23 6NT, England

The graphic circle C logo is a registered trademark of David C Cook.

The website addresses recommended throughout this book are offered as a
resource to you. These websites are not intended in any way to be or imply an
endorsement on the part of David C Cook, nor do we vouch for their content.

Unless otherwise noted, all Scripture quotations are taken from The Holy Bible,
English Standard Version* (ESV*), copyright © 2001 by Crossway, a publishing
ministry of Good News Publishers. Used by permission. All rights reserved. Scripture
quotations marked KJV are taken from the King James Version of the Bible. (Public
Domain.) Scripture quotations marked NIV are taken from the Holy Bible, New
International Version*, NIV*. Copyright © 1973, 2011 by Biblica, Inc.™ Used by
permission of Zondervan. All rights reserved worldwide. www.zondervan.com.

The author has added italics to Scripture quotations for emphasis.

LCCN 2014945718
ISBN 978-1-4347-0773-4
eISBN 978-1-4347-0857-1

© 2014 Samuel Kee
Published in association with the literary agency of The
Gates Group, www.the-gates-group.com.

The Team: Alex Field, Steve Parolini, Amy Konyndyk,
Nick Lee, Jack Campbell, Karen Athen
Cover Design: Faceout Studios, Charles Brock

Printed in the United States of America
First Edition 2014

1 2 3 4 5 6 7 8 9 10

080114

To Shanté

CONTENTS

ACKNOWLEDGMENTS

Thank you, Shanté, for believing in me and encouraging me to write. You do an amazing job at holding down the fort while I'm in the bunker. Carson and Gleason, you are so patient with me during this process and take so much interest. You are the best boys!

Thank you, Don Gates, for being a wonderful advocate. It is a great blessing to know you and see your gifts in action. Your work on this book has made it come to life. You have given me feet.

Thank you, Tim Augustyn, for your friendship. You sat through hundreds of cups of coffee with me, as we dreamed about ideas and books, most recently this one. Thanks for carefully reading anything that I gave you. You helped shape the chapters and offered helpful edits along the way.

Thank you, Steve Parolini, for your work on the manuscript. You are truly gifted. You kept me on track and got rid of all the boring parts (any that are left are my fault!). Thank you for caring for this project.

Thank you, Jack Campbell, for going through the manuscript with such precision. You have given my ideas more clarity. I marvel at your attention to detail and efficiency with words. You have done a fine job polishing this book.

Thank you, North Suburban Church, for all your support and for giving me the chance to write. It is an honor to be a part of this community of Christ. Your enthusiasm is contagious.

Thank you, Alex Field and David C Cook, for having a vision for this book and making it possible. Thanks also to Amy Konyndyk, Nick Lee, and Karen Athen for being a part of the team. Your creativity and commitment have been wonderful.

THE PARLOR CHAIR IS OPEN

She flicked her cigarette nervously, checked her phone, and exhaled a dancing stream of smoke. She was too small for her denim jacket, sitting on the curb outside the tattoo shop. She had a shock of red hair that sharply contrasted with the drab parking lot. Her name was Julianne. She was waiting for the artist to complete his drawings. He was inside the tattoo shop, sitting at a drafting desk, the long arm of a magnifying lamp stretched over his paper as he drew in purple ink.

Another man lay shirtless on a tattoo bed, face buried in the headrest, trying not to cry. A female tattoo artist was working on his back. She had a white cloth in her left hand and a tattoo gun in her right. Her hands moved rhythmically back and forth between drawing and wiping, drawing and wiping. The gun hummed like barber shop clippers. Under the table, her foot pressed a small, circular pedal like a seamstress with a sewing machine. Only she wasn't sewing thread into fabric, but ink into skin. She chatted effortlessly with the receptionist at the front desk as the big man on her table gripped the edge of his vinyl bed in obvious pain.

"I'm getting this tattoo for my dad," Julianne said to me outside the shop. "He died a few weeks ago, and I am getting it as a memorial to him." She swiped at her iPhone a few times, then held it out to me. "Here's the picture I'm getting."

I looked at the image on her phone. Her eyes met mine, searching for approval. I smiled. She showed me the spot where the tattoo
would go, hovering a hand over her leg. It would be a large tattoo,
taking up most of her thigh. I figured this girl couldn't be much older
than twenty. She still needed her daddy.

"This was his," she said, proudly tugging the edges of the denim
jacket. Its sleeves were cut off and it was decorated with Harley-
Davidson patches. "I know it's too big for me, but I'm a daddy's girl
and it helps me to feel him all around me." She closed her eyes, as if
she were in the middle of one of the hugs he used to give her.

Through the glass doors, beyond the sign that read "18 and over
only," her artist was preparing his station.

It is a world that's easily recognizable to those who have been
touched by it, but perhaps mysterious to those who haven't. It's a
world where artist and physician collide. The artist will recognize
the sheets of paper, the full-color spectrum of ink, the sketches,
stencils, and markers. The physician will recognize the sterile
needles, rubber gloves, folding tables, razors, and sanitation soap.
The walls are covered with artwork and mirrors and old tattoo
paraphernalia. Each station has been personalized, like an office
cubicle, with family pictures and decorations particular to its artist. Whereas a doctor attempts to heal the body by repairing its
brokenness, the tattoo artist heals the soul by recording its longings
on the surface of the skin. The client and the artist work together
to create the image, making each one a unique collaboration of
personality and artistry.

Julianne smashed her cigarette on the curb and stood up.
Touching her leg, she said, "It's time." She turned around toward

the shop and let out one more mouthful of smoke. Her parlor chair
was open.

THEY TELL A STORY

Tattooists are a voice for today's culture. They reveal the desires
of a nation transposed onto the skin in plain sight. Tattoos used
to be almost exclusively frightening or menacing, but that perception is changing. A 2006 survey by the Pew Research Center
shows that 40 percent of Americans who are under the age of
forty have at least one tattoo.[1] A 2011 article by the *Washington
Post* reports that tattoos have gone mainstream.[2] Tattoo shops are
more common today than ever before, and tattoos themselves
are hip. You'll find tattoos on your sports heroes (think LeBron
James), at your local bookstore (*The Girl with the Dragon Tattoo*),
and decorating your local barista (coffee shops are great places to
find tattoos).

While we may get tattoos for many reasons, there's one common purpose: to tell a story. Perhaps to tell *the* story, the story of
our humanity. Tattoos are a way of permanently recording one's
sense of dignity, lest we forget. With permanent ink, we remember a feeling, a person, an experience, a love, a victory, a loss. All
the stuff that makes us *feel* our humanity.

Once while I was getting a haircut, my barber's wrist slipped
in front of my eyes, revealing a tattoo of a patch. I asked her to
tell me about it. She hesitated. I said, "You're probably going to
say that it was random, but I don't accept that answer." With a
smile I added, "So what's the story behind it?"

She confessed, "You're right, I *was* going to tell you that it was random; that's what I tell everyone. But it's not. It has a lot of meaning." She told me that she hadn't spoken to her mother for five years, even though she had a son now, whom her mom had never met. Mom was bipolar, abusive, and unstable. "When I was a kid, she used to call me her little rag doll—you know, the kind with the patches on it, like on the elbows and knees?" I told her I knew exactly what she was talking about. "Well," she continued, "I got tattoos of patches, just like a rag doll's patches, to remind me that I'm still my mom's little rag doll." She pointed to her legs and arms and said shyly, "I have more patches here, here, and here."

These tattoos were an attempt to cling to the lost love of her mother, bringing it right to the surface as a constant reminder that her mom used to cherish her. Every patch said, "I'm still worth it to her." I couldn't escape the irony, however, that the best she could do was think of herself as a rag doll. It was a novice attempt at repainting a deeper work on her soul.

REPAINTING THE MASTERS

When I was first learning to paint, I would try to copy the masters. I'd study paintings such as *Starry Night, View of Toledo,* or *American Gothic,* then try to copy them stroke for stroke. But my lines were never as good, my colors never as bright, my forms never as gripping. Though my pictures were an attempt at recreating the real thing, they were not the real thing—not even close.

Tattoos are like the paintings of a novice trying to recreate the work of a master. The real Master, God, has painted us with dignity, life, and worth. Each of God's paintings is a masterpiece in every sense of the word. Only God's paintings aren't done on canvas—not even the canvas of our skin—but on the human soul. The Master has left his mark on every human soul, hidden beneath the surface, and tattoos are one of our desperate attempts to repaint what we sense is beneath. Every skin tattoo falls short of the real thing, but at least tattoos are trying to get at the real thing. Tattoos are tributes to and trophies of what it means to be human.

THE ARMAMENT OF THE SOUL

Louie Zamperini survived enemy bullets, crashing planes, near drowning, sharks, starvation, and forty-seven days drifting on a shoddy raft in the Pacific Ocean, where he lived on fish blood and bird guts. But compared to what he was about to endure, all of that was easy. Having lost half of his body weight and avoided death on several fronts, it seemed that this WWII airman could survive anything. Then he was taken prisoner, and what he experienced as a POW would leave him reeling in ways he never imagined possible.

You might think that facing sharks for forty-seven days, nearly starving to death, seeing your friends slaughtered, and being attacked by a fighter plane while you're floating in an unarmed raft, already half-baked from the sun, would be the worst possible things you'd ever have to endure. But Louie, as documented by Laura Hillenbrand in her 2010 book, *Unbroken*, discovered something even more harrowing: the loss of dignity. At least when he was starving, he still retained his humanity. At least when he was fighting the sharks, he was still fighting. But when his enemies began to spit on him, put his face in feces, and treat him like an animal, he nearly broke. Nothing else caused him to ponder suicide like the loss of his dignity. Hillenbrand wrote:

> The crash of [their plane] *Green Hornet* had left Louie and [his friend] Phil in the most desperate physical extremity, without food, water, or shelter. But on Kwajalein, the guards sought to deprive them of something that had sustained them even as all else had been lost: dignity. This self-respect and sense of self-worth, the innermost armament of the soul, lies at the heart of humanness; to be deprived of it is to be dehumanized, to be cleaved from, and cast below, mankind. Men subjected to dehumanizing treatment experience profound wretchedness and loneliness and find that hope is almost impossible to retain. Without dignity, identity is erased. In its absence, men are defined not by themselves, but by their captors and the circumstances in which they are forced to live.[3]

Yes, in order to survive, humans need essentials such as air, food, water, shelter, and clothing, but they also need dignity. Dignity is crucial to survival. Without it, the human soul dies. And when your soul is dead, your body longs to follow. Dignity is essential to humanity; it is the "armament of the soul." To remove people's dignity is to discard their humanity, to trample their lives and worth in the muck, to leave them unprotected from despair. Louie learned this about dignity:

The stubborn retention of it, even in the face of extreme physical hardship, can hold a man's soul in his body long past the point at which the body should have surrendered it. The loss of it can carry a man off as surely as thirst, hunger, exposure, and asphyxiation, and with greater cruelty. In places like Kwajalein, degradation could be as lethal as a bullet.[4]

DEEPER THAN SCARS

But the sharks still circle, hunger still comes, and people still are cruel. What then? Is it possible to find a source of dignity that runs deeper than our scars? Is it possible to find a source of permanent significance? What if I were to tell you that *everyone* has these kinds of indestructible tattoos? These tattoos run much deeper, so deep that they're untouchable. They are written on your soul in indelible ink and can never be erased.

They are soul tattoos, put there by the hand of the Master.

And the best gallery in which to see them is exile. We all have our own POW camps and our own prison guards. The metanarrative, the overarching story, of humanity is one of exile. We are all displaced, discouraged, defeated, and dominated—and some of us feel it more than others. We are adrift in the middle of a shark-infested ocean, crying out to be rescued from drowning, waiting for someone to throw us a lifeline.

It is in this place of desperation where we most clearly see the stains that run deeper than the scars. Here, where we're stripped of everything that enables us to remain self-dependent and blind, we find clarity. Only when we lose ourselves can we find ourselves. Then we are able to see the tattoos on our souls that tell us of our beginning, purpose, worth, calling, and love.

I have this crazy idea that tattooed on your soul are permanent stories of who you are, which you must see if you're going to know true dignity. Yes, every tattoo has a story, but also, every story has tattoos. And they don't come from what you've accomplished or what has been handed to you by others. These tattoos come from another hand.

GOD'S TATS AND OURS

Tattoos can be found in the Bible, and on the Person you'd least expect. In the ancient Hebrew book of Isaiah, we read about tattoos on the very hands of God. Here's what the Lord said: "Behold, I have engraved you on the palms of my hands" (Isa. 49:16).

This verse recalls the ancient Near East practice of drawing pictures on the skin by puncturing its surface. The symbolism of such a practice is best represented by modern-day tattoos. It seems that God has tattooed the names of his people on his hands. This is a good place to start. We must first examine God's tattoos if we're going to be able to see our own.

From the same Hebrew book, we will discover four tattoos that God has punctured into our souls. Each tattoo is a story from God, an eternity of dignity in a world of insanity. As your lungs take in each breath, I want you to start training your thoughts on these tattoos, found in Isaiah 43:1–7. Ready? *Inhale.* "You are mine." *Exhale.* *Inhale.* "I will be with you." *Exhale. Inhale.* "I love you." *Exhale.*

Inhale. "I created you for my glory." *Exhale.* These four soul tattoos, engraved by the hand of the Master, are the true source of our dignity.

NOT WHAT YOU NEED

The mighty Google search engine is mightier than we think, for its results are tailored to the individual. So if I type "orange" into Google on my computer, it will yield different results than if you typed it on yours. My search results will be based on my previous Internet activity, age, location, gender, interests, language, and so forth. Google is designed to provide answers not only to our inquiries but also to our interests. It gives us what it thinks we want and not just what we ask for. Our "objective" searches are actually quite subjective.

While this can be helpful, it can also be toxic. Consider this line from Coldplay's song "Fix You": "When you try your best, but you don't succeed. When you get what you want, but not what you need."[5] I find this very telling. It doesn't take too much brainpower to comprehend that our needs are different than our wants and that too much of the latter can destroy us. For example, though I may want an endless supply of cash, fame, or buffets, I probably don't need them—unless I really want to be stingy, secluded, or stout. Ironically, too much of any "freedom" actually leads to imprisonment. You become a slave to what you most want. And if you're the slave, the object of your desire is your taskmaster, oftentimes working you to death. We all know what that feels like. Maybe our lives are the way they are because we've been chasing our wants instead of our needs.

Google, you leave us with gaping blind spots. You keep the spotlight on us, while the surrounding world of possibilities remains in the dark, unsearched. You give me more of me. I don't need more of me. I need a solution that is outside of me, unlike me, and not so narrow-minded. I don't need more of my same biases and gender stereotypes. I don't need to be electrocuted by the cultural brainwave, as it zaps away the deep and ancient, leaving me with only the shallow and modern.

EXILE

So let me transport you out of the clutches of Google, out of the grip of cultural ethnocentrism, and out of the grasp of pop culture, iThis and iThat. We're going to a place and time far, far away, to a strange people in a strange land bearing the weight of a strange situation. We're going to ancient Israel, to a voice crying in the wilderness nearly twenty-five hundred years ago. Here we will find a people who have been taken captive by an oppressive nation. They have been conquered, captured, and enslaved, and they're not sure if they will ever make it home again. They don't know if anyone really cares, if God is really there, or if they even have a prayer. Israel is in exile.

A pagan and violent culture that glorifies war surrounds these people. For fun, the kings throw them into an arena and release lions and armed soldiers to chase and kill them. For worship, the kings sentence the people's sons and daughters to be burned to death as sacrifices to their gods.

Welcome to Babylon.

Though ancient Israel is very different from modern society, if you look beneath the surface, you'll see the same tattoos. You'll see the same scars and struggles and fears. You'll see yourself.

The book of Isaiah was written both to condemn sin and to comfort sinners. The plotline of Isaiah goes something like this: *Though God's people fail, God's Servant will prevail.* How did they fail? First, they failed to stay true to their God. They were blind (42:19), inattentive (v. 20), falling short (v. 22), radically disobedient (v. 24), and insensitive (v. 25). Second, they failed because their homeland was destroyed. Here they found themselves in Babylon, defeated, dominated, discouraged, and displaced. They felt every sharp and lonely edge of the word *exile.*

Though God's people fail, God's Servant prevails. Isaiah, notwithstanding their present situation, told his people their circumstances wouldn't have the last say. I find the mouthful-of-a-word *notwithstanding* to be an ocean of comfort. It means "despite the fact of" or "though you would have expected this to be the case, actually *this* is the case." Though you are in exile, you can hold on to hope. Despite the fact that your scars are real and painful, God has not left you.

Notwithstanding your enemies, the parlor chair is open.

TATTOO 1

YOU ARE MINE

CHAPTER 1

YOU CAME OUT OF MY HEAD

But now thus says the Lord, *he who created you, O Jacob, he who formed you, O Israel: "Fear not, for I have redeemed you; I have called you by name, you are mine."*

Isaiah 43:1

HIS CLAIM

There's no way to get a tattoo solely from a machine. You also need an artist, someone to wield the machine. Someone who will touch you, pierce your skin. In an age of mass production and one size fits all, tattoos refuse to comply. They are rebels. Every tattoo is hand-made, created by an artist. Like the creations of all artists, the work of tattooists is deeply personal. But unlike other artists, tattoo artists can't sell their work independent of human beings; each tattoo either lives or dies with its recipient. It is art that melts into our lives; or maybe our lives soak up the art.

Tattoos are knotted with the human body, dependent on human skin while simultaneously laying claim to it. In a way, the tattoo artist lays claim to the person receiving the tattoo as well. Everyone who gets a tattoo is left with a permanent reminder of the artist who touched his or her life.

God is the ultimate tattoo artist, but his canvas goes deeper than skin. He stitches tattoos to the soul. One such tattoo reads, "You are mine." This is a permanent-ink truth that no exile can erase. We are God's through creation, formation, redemption, and calling. Here's how Isaiah put it: "But now thus says the LORD, he who created you, O Jacob, he who formed you, O Israel: 'Fear not, for I have redeemed you; I have called you by name, you are mine'" (Isa. 43:1).

The little phrase "but now" means notwithstanding all the reasons you think God might be bogus or against you, he is actually laying claim to you. Notwithstanding your scars, there is a stain that runs deeper. This is the first soul tattoo, written on every person who reads these words and even on those who don't. Despite your expectations and experiences, God has copyrighted you as his own masterpiece.

God looks at you and says, "You are mine." He's put this tattoo on your soul so you will never forget it.

HELLO, I AM GOD

You'd think an encounter with the God of the universe might be a particularly unforgettable experience. But history tells us God's people were often forgetting him. God needed to reintroduce himself more than a few times to his people.

The original creation story (Gen. 1–2) was written for the Egyptian slaves, the Israelites who had been in captivity for four hundred years. As Israel was coming out of Egypt, in what was known as the exodus, God spoke to Moses, the leader of the Israelites. Moses recorded God's words in what we now know as the first five books in the Bible, also called the Pentateuch. The Israelites finally escaping Egyptian slavery desperately needed to hear what Moses had to say about their Creator.

Upon leaving Egypt, the Israelites would soon encounter many other gods and creation stories, which they would have to sort through. Also, they were experiencing the strain of a national identity crisis. Given all their trauma and uncertainty, they needed to know one crucial thing: their Maker. They needed to hear about the God who made them by his powerful word, controlled the cosmos, and separated light from dark. So he gave them Genesis.

Fast-forward thousands of years to the sixth century BC and to the book of Isaiah, which tells a somewhat familiar story of slavery and a new exodus. This time Babylon was the taskmaster from which they needed a new exodus. That's why the prophet Isaiah comforted the lonely exiles the way that he did. That's why the prophet went right to the source of everything—to creation. Above all, they needed to hear about the one who created them and possessed them.

If you suffer from exile for too long, you risk losing national and personal dignity. You forget that you're a blessed people. You lose track of your origin—your Creator. And then you become groundless.

One of the most important things I can do for people who are experiencing an "exile" of sorts is to give them a sense of belonging, help them see their connection to their Creator. What is your exile? What is holding you captive? Though circumstances often suggest otherwise, we don't belong to our captors; their grip is weak. We belong to the God who says, "You are mine."

THE LION

The children were enveloped in darkness. There was no light, no landscape, no living thing. Not even dust or wind. They didn't know where they were in this strange new world with neither smell nor sensation. Digory and Polly had entered this world after putting on a magical ring, which had the ability to transport its wearers into other realms. Before they could process the emptiness, they began to hear a song in the distance. Astounded, they found that the song was coming from the mouth of a lion!

The Lion's song was both powerful and beautiful. When it tumbled around the empty space, life-forms began to appear. First dirt appeared and then grass. Hills were shaped mysteriously before their eyes. Trees began to burst out of the new earth, followed by animals and every living thing that belonged in paradise. C. S. Lewis wrote in *The Magician's Nephew*:

> Polly was finding the song more and more interesting because she thought she was beginning to see the connection between the music and the things that were happening. When a line of dark firs sprang up on a ridge about a hundred yards away she felt that they were connected with a series of deep, prolonged notes which the Lion had sung a second before. And when he burst into a rapid series of lighter notes she was not surprised to see primroses suddenly appearing in every direction. Thus, with an unspeakable thrill, she felt quite

certain that all the things were coming (as she said) "Out of the Lion's head." When you listened to his song you heard the things he was making up: when you looked round you, you saw them. This was so exciting that she had no time to be afraid.[1]

I love the idea that all things come "out of the Lion's head." Were it not for the Lion, there would be nothing. The Lion in Lewis's story represents God. From stories like this and from the Bible, we learn about the act of creation, the Actor of creation, and the product of creation. We'll consider all three of these in this chapter.

Recall God's claim "You are mine." How can he say this? God can claim us because we came out of his head. "But now thus says the LORD, he who created you, O Jacob … you are mine" (Isa. 43:1).

When God spoke his mighty word, he created life. He didn't use any ingredients to make the world, only his word. He didn't grab a fistful of dust or a handful of hydrogen. Before he created, there was neither dust nor hydrogen. There was absolutely nothing, something so astounding that we struggle to imagine it. Before God sang his song of creation, there was nothing but God. All was God and God was all. Only when he began to announce his creative word did the elements burst onto the scene. Actually, he had to create the scene, too!

ONLY GOD CREATES

The universe was created ex nihilo, or "out of nothing." Hebrews 11:3 says, "By faith we understand that the universe was created by the word of God, so that what is seen was not made out of things that are visible." Nothing predates God.

This fact alone has staggering implications for your life. It means that if anything is here in this world, it's because God brought it here, singing it into existence. The Bible affirms this by its use of the word *bara*, which is the Hebrew verb for "create." *Bara* occurs nearly seventy times in the Hebrew Scriptures, and every time God is the subject. Not once does anything or anyone else have the privilege of being the subject of the verb "create." Other gods are never the subject of *bara*. Circumstances are never the subject of *bara*. Natural forces are never the subject of *bara*. Humans are never the subject of *bara*. Idols and possessions are never the subject of *bara*.

This means that if anything is here in this world, not only did God bring it here, but also he *wanted* it here. Maybe you need to read that last sentence again. For if you're here, living and breathing, there's only one reason why: God wanted you here. You are no accident; you were not created by random elements; you were not a mistake. God sang you into this world by his powerful word and will. You can never say that no one wants you here, because God would beg to differ. You can't erase the soul tattoo that says "You are mine."

NEED VERSUS WANT

There's a big difference between need and want, even when it comes to God. God did not need to create you; he wanted to. God did not need you to be here; he wanted you to be here. God's aseity—a fancy word meaning that God's existence is in and from himself—assures us that he did not create us out of lack. His existence did not depend on ours. Trace the beginning of all the beginnings back to the beginning and what do you find? A being who does not require anything else to be complete. In order for the appearance of the material world to make any sense, we must accept that this being started it all.

We must grasp this in order to drown in God's love. Many of us are only up to our ankles in it; some might be up to their knees. Unless we encounter the fact that God did not need us but *wanted* us, creating us out of his full, free will, we'll never experience the marvel of his love. If God didn't need us, then why did he create us? He created us so that he might give us his love.

Consider adoption. Although they already had three children, my parents started fostering a little boy when I was three years old. They thought it would be meaningful if we provided a home to a boy who didn't have one. Well, we fell in love with that little boy and ended up adopting him. Brian officially became my brother when we were in the second grade together. His last name changed from King to Kee.

My parents didn't need another mouth to feed or child to raise. It was not as if this little boy would add to their financial portfolio. In every way, as do all children, this little boy would actually drain the family resources. So why did my parents adopt? They adopted because they *wanted* another child.

In a sense, the old, unwanted King is gone and now only the new, wanted Kee remains. My brother gets to live the rest of his life knowing that someone wants him. How cool is that? And that's the way it is with us and God too. Everyone God creates is created out of want, not need. And we get to live the rest of our lives knowing that.

YOU ARE VERY GOOD

At the same time that we see God's end in us, we must also see our end in him. What is the goal and purpose of creation? A verse in the New Testament helps us capture both: "All things were created through him and for him" (Col. 1:16).

This verse claims that God created all things. Think back to the first pages of the Bible. There we see the joyful Lion, singing out the world from his mouth, ex nihilo. We see God's delight in creation as he called it "good" and even "very good" (Gen. 1:31). God looked at the masterpiece his word had created and exclaimed, "This is wonderful! This is perfect!"

Contrast this joyful view of creation with the ancient Greeks' beliefs. According to Greek and other philosophical systems, the physical world was fundamentally evil. Matter didn't matter! It was nothing to fawn over. All of creation, including by extension you and me, was nothing to celebrate. The Bible, however, boldly states that creation is good—very good, in fact. Creation is God's achievement in which he takes great pleasure. "May the glory of the LORD endure forever; may the LORD rejoice in his works" (Ps. 104:31).

Some of us have been scarred by the thought *I don't matter.* Thankfully, that is not what God thinks. He rejoices over you and calls you his own. You matter to him.

The second part of Colossians 1:16 states, "All things were created through him and *for him.*" Creation is meant to serve and glorify God. To be created by God means that we are also created *for* him. We're to be a huge neon arrow that points to God.

CUT FLOWERS

Nonetheless, we've been damaged. The neon arrow has shorted out, only flickering now and again. Though creation was meant to be a constant witness to the God who made it, creation has fallen. That includes you and me. We have fallen away from the Source of life and are suffering from death.

We might look radiant and vibrant on the outside, but don't be fooled. Whenever I bring my wife flowers, I'm reminded of this truth. Because what are flowers anyway? Severed plants. Happy Valentine's Day. Oh, we buy them a little more time by sticking them in water, but that's just a temporary reprieve from certain death. They've been cut off from their life source. They'll have beauty for a little while, but it will soon fade. The petals will begin to fall off, the leaves will begin to wilt, and the head of the flower will bow in defeat. What traces of residual energy it had will soon disappear.

We're all like cut flowers. We have traces of energy and life that will get us by for a little while, maybe seventy-five years or so, but then our petals will fall to the table and we'll bow our heads in defeat. All of creation has been cut off from its life source. That is why we see constant suffering and death around us; these are symptoms of our massive plight. We have to find a way to be reconnected to the root, the life Source, before it's too late. We need the Lion to return to his creation and put life back together.

I knew that whenever my parents said, "Samuel John Kee!" I was probably in trouble. By stating my full name, they reminded me that they didn't just give me life (and a name) but that they also had authority over me. God did the same for his people when he said, "But now thus says the LORD, he who created you, O Jacob, he who formed you, O Israel … you are mine" (Isa. 43:1). In a sense, God was calling his people by their full name, using both "Jacob" and "Israel." He wanted them to know how serious he was and that he had authority over them as their Creator. In the same way, God wants us to know without question that we belong to him through creation.

CHAPTER 2

MEET THE ARTIST

But now thus says the LORD, he who created you, O Jacob,
he who formed you, O Israel: "Fear not, for I have redeemed
you; I have called you by name, you are mine."

Isaiah 43:1

CREATION AND FORMATION

God can say to us "You are mine" because he created us. The reason we exist is because he wants us to exist. But why does he want us here? God didn't create us in order to ditch us, though some might think so. God created us so that he can make something out of us. God is an artist who plans with his heart what he fashions with his hands. Consider the next part of Isaiah 43:1, "he who formed you, O Israel."

Not only does God create us, but also he forms us. To create is to generate the raw materials, while to form is to fashion the raw materials into something specific. Using clay as an analogy, to create would be to produce the clay, while to form would be to shape it into a useful vessel. This means that just as we belong to God by creation, we also belong to him by formation.

This is crucial for us to understand, for I've observed that the very process that was meant to show us the hand of God has caused many people to be blind to it. The term *formation* has been dumped for other words, such as *setback* and *misfortune*. The beautiful process by which God forms us, driving us deeper into his possession, has been sterilized and stripped of significance and intimacy. To put it plainly, we see trials and challenges in life as evidence of God's abandonment. But for God's children, nothing could be further from the truth. Our suffering is not a sign that God has abandoned us; it's an indication that the Artist is at work in our lives.

POTTERY

The Hebrew word for "form" used in Isaiah 43:1 is *yatsar*. *Yatsar*, which is also the root word behind the English word *reworked*, means to shape something into form by pressing, squeezing, and putting it under distress. The potter takes a lump of clay and makes it into something for his use. Consider this verse from Scripture: "So I went down to the potter's house, and there he was working at his wheel. And the vessel he was making of clay was spoiled in the potter's hand, and he reworked it into another vessel, as it seemed good to the potter to do" (Jer. 18:3–4).

The patient potter was working and reworking his vessel until it was just as he wanted it to be. A couple of verses later, we read, "Behold, like the clay in the potter's hand, so are you in my hand, O house of Israel" (v. 6). God is the Potter, and his people are the clay. In Isaiah's book, this same metaphor is again used to describe God's relationship with his people: "Shall the potter be regarded as the clay, that … the thing formed say of him who formed it, 'He has no understanding'?" (Isa. 29:16).

I come from a family of artists. My sister Tiffany has a master's degree in art and is a gifted art teacher. My sister Emily majored in fashion design and has ample artistic abilities and vision. My third sister, Allison, has also dabbled in art in college and is quite talented. I myself am not totally inept with a paintbrush, and I've been around enough studios to know about pottery. Pottery is not for the weak or undisciplined, to say the least. It's a full body experience, one that will test your patience and emotions. Just hearing some of the terms that potters use will help you understand and appreciate the process a bit more: *throwing, pushing, pulling, cutting, squeezing, spinning, smacking, karate chopping, pounding, working, pressuring,* and *firing.*

God is the Potter, and we are the clay. With that in mind, take a look at that list of words again. Ouch! We start off as a lump. Then he has to make sure that we don't have any impurities. He has to wrangle out all the air bubbles and smooth us out. Like all potters, God has to get us into the right condition before he'll ever put us on his wheel. This is a process called wedging. The potter will pound on the clay, over and over again, to mix it and purify it. Some potters repeatedly throw the clay down on a hard surface until it is pure, soft, and usable. Our Potter will squeeze us, roll us, twist us, and press us. And that's just the beginning.

When all this is done, he puts us on his wheel for a process known as throwing. Do you like the sound of that? I don't! The Potter slams a lump of clay down onto the wheel in order first to "center" us. This is a crucial step; otherwise, the motion of the wheel will destroy us against the Potter's hands rather than shape us *within* the Potter's hands. To center the clay, the Potter must lean over the spinning wheel and put his weight on it. He must brace his elbows against his hips and place one hand over the clay and one hand beside the clay. With one hand he will push the clay down and with the other he will push the clay forward. All the while, the clay is spinning at a high rate on the wheel.

Once the clay is perfectly centered, the Potter will begin to shape us, digging his thumbs into our core, pulling out our sides, over and over again. He pushes, pulls, and wipes. He uses pressure, lifts up, and expands out. He drags a knife along the side, puts a sponge in the middle, and adds water to keep us moist. He does all this with perfect patience and precision, because one jitter could send the whole thing flying, splattering us against the walls.

Having shaped us just how he wants us to be, the Potter signs us with his name and then puts us in the kiln to be fired. After spending time in the furnace, we'll be glazed and fired again, a second time. This is not a quick process, but takes days and days.

But this is where the analogy falls short, because unlike the pottery, which receives its final shape after the kiln, God continues to form his people throughout their lives. Our formation is a lifelong process; God does not end his work on us and then put us in the cupboard. He keeps working on us.

From this, two things stand out to me. First, God is in absolute control of all life and history. That was what the prophet Isaiah wanted the people of Israel to know in the midst of their trials. But second, God works patiently and lovingly on his people, making them into something special for his use.

THIS IS WHO I AM

I met a guy from Chicago named Cola. He had several tattoos on his arms, which he proudly told me about. There were three in particular that he wanted me to see. The first was of his kids' names. The second was of a music staff and some notes. The third was a tattoo of the Chicago Bulls logo. I asked why these three tattoos in particular were so important to him. "This is who I am," he replied. He had a "take it or leave it" look on his face. These were the things that meant the world to him, the things that made him who he was. A lot of people get tattoos for this reason: to reaffirm or establish identity. They tattoo on the outside the things that mean the most on the inside.

Before we condescendingly brush this aside as mere sentimentality, as if we're so much more than kids, entertainment, or city pride, I'd like to suggest that Cola is not far from the truth. In one sense, he's exactly right. The things he honors with his tattoos have shaped him and made him into the kind of person he is today. The Bible supports this understanding with its use of the word *yatsar*. Recall from chapter 1 that the Hebrew word for "create," *bara*, has only one subject, God. Only God creates things out of nothing. In contrast, the word *yatsar* has many subjects. All sorts of things can be the subject of the verb "form." This is significant.

It means that many things in this life can mold us, shape us, and make us who we are. Ultimately God the Potter is the one who shapes us. However, God uses many things in our lives to shape us, even things such as entertainment and city pride. Just as a potter uses many different tools to shape the clay, God uses countless experiences, abilities, relationships, and possessions to shape his people into a specific design—his design. Those who tattoo their so-called identity on their skin are merely lifting the lid of God's toolbox for others to see.

So what are some of the things that have shaped you? What tools has the Potter used with you, pushing you gently, purifying you, or pounding you into shape? While in graduate school, I was required by a counseling class to write a paper about five things in my life that had shaped me the most. My list included things that were both good and bad, abilities that I had, things that were out of my control, and people God had brought into my life. Take a moment to come up with your own list of five things that have shaped you the most. Do you see the Potter's hand on that list?

POSSESSION

There's an expression we use when describing something that has gone from one condition to another. Picture a rickety, run-down house. Your friend moves into it and begins to work on it. Using all her tools and talents, she renovates it, inside and out. After all the work is done and you visit her, what do you say? "You have really made this place your own!" Why do we spend so much time and effort on renovation? Because we couldn't care less about the old, run-down shack? Hardly! We spend our energy on the things we want to make our own—on the things that we love and want to possess.

The potter spends time with the clay because he wants to make it his own. Before, it was just a lump of dirt, worth little to anyone. But he invests in it. The more he works on it, the more it becomes his own. The more he pounds on it, stretches it, and shapes it, the more he possesses it. Can you see the connection between the soul tattoo

"You are mine" and formation? *Formation drives us deeper into posses-sion.* The more God works on us, the more we become his. The more he forms us, the more he can claim us—or, if you like, the more it can be said that God has really made this place his own.

You are a "place" that God wants to make his own, but you're going to need a little renovation. This isn't just a helpful metaphor; it's a rather vivid truth. While God used to dwell in houses made with hands (the temple of Old Testament times, for example), since the coming of the Holy Spirit, God has made his home in his people. In *you.* So the reno-vation imagery is right on target. "Or do you not know that your body is a temple of the Holy Spirit within you?" (1 Cor. 6:19).

God begins his renovation by saving us from the penalty of our sin, but he doesn't stop there. After giving his life for ours, he begins to cleanse us of our sins. Here's how the apostle Paul put it: "Christ loved the church and gave himself up for her, that he might sanctify her, having cleansed her by the washing of water with the word, so that he might present the church to himself in splendor, without spot or wrinkle or any such thing, that she might be holy and with-out blemish" (Eph. 5:25–27).

God continues to spin us around on his wheel, working out our blemishes, making us his own. Because he loves us enough to form us, he is able to say, "You are mine." I pray that you can see how your trials are not a sign of abandonment but a signal of renovation.

WRESTLING

Has God been working on you all these years? Has your life been constantly spinning? Do you know what it's like to be stretched and pulled almost to the point where you think that everything will fly apart? Trials don't mean you are less of God's treasure, but more. The more you allow him to work on you, the more you become his. I know there are times when this might be hard to believe, but there is another reason to trust that trials are a signal God is at work in your life. Read what Isaiah had to say below. Notice the change of names as the verbs shift from "created" to "formed." "But now thus says the LORD, he who created you, O Jacob, he who formed you, O Israel" (Isa. 43:1).

God *created* Jacob, but he *formed* Israel. What is the difference? There were two miraculous interventions behind the birth of Jacob. With God's help, Isaac met and married Rebekah. Genesis 24 makes it clear that this was an act of God. However, having children was not easy for Isaac and Rebekah, for Rebekah was barren (Gen. 25:21). Isaac prayed to the Lord, and "the LORD granted his prayer, and Rebekah his wife conceived" (v. 21). Inasmuch as Rebekah conceived a child, God had created Jacob in her womb. Yes, God created the child Jacob, just as God creates every other child.

But God *formed* Israel. If you're familiar with Jacob, you'll know that God changed his name to Israel. Why did God change Jacob's name and under what circumstances did he change it? The answers to these questions help us to see the connection between God's shaping of us and our deeper possession within him.

In Genesis 32:22–32, we discover the event during which God changed Jacob's name. It was a wrestling match. "And Jacob was left alone. And a man wrestled with him until the breaking of the day.... [The man] touched his hip socket, and Jacob's hip was put out of joint as he wrestled with him" (vv. 24–25).

In the middle of this wrestling match, Jacob asked God to bless him. God did not respond with immediate blessing, but instead he asked Jacob a question, "What is your name?" (v. 27). When Jacob told God his name, God said, "Your name shall no longer be called Jacob, but Israel, for you have striven with God and with men, and have prevailed" (v. 28). The name Israel means essentially "the one who strives with God." More pointedly, it means *"the one who wrestles with God."*

Now let's return to our verse, Isaiah 43:1, and read the phrase again, "he who formed you, O Israel." Since we know what the word "form" means, it's easy to see that it sounds a lot like a wrestling match, doesn't it? God was forming Jacob, as a potter forms the clay. God wrestled with him, pushing and pulling at him, throwing him and pounding him. In the end, God knocked Jacob's hip out of socket as a lasting remembrance of the new "shape" he'd be in after encountering God on the mat.

I grew up wrestling. I wrestled from elementary school through college. Wrestling is not a metaphor to me. It's a visceral memory. I know what it's like to circle an opponent, each of us wanting to take the other to the mat. One inevitably does, and then the struggle to escape begins. Holding a man down is a lot harder than being held down. Wrestling, especially in college, is a fight—a beautiful fight. I wish more people knew how many thousands of calculations, adjustments, and plans go on in a single wrestling match; it's a physical chess game. Most of all, wrestling is intimate. Flesh on flesh, sweat on sweat. Muscle to muscle, bone to bone, head to head. In Jacob's case, the Potter was in one corner of the ring, and the clay was in the other. The Potter wrestled the clay; the clay was forever marked by the hands of the Potter. Israel was defined by the fact that he had wrestled with God.

God could have proposed a game of checkers. Or, as in that comical scene in *The Princess Bride*, God could have suggested a game of "to the wit." He could have challenged Jacob to a footrace or a duel with swords. But he didn't. God didn't propose any kind of contest that would put them at a distance from each other; he proposed a contest that would lead them directly into each other's arms.

But why? Because God had plans for Israel. God chose Israel out of all the nations to be his chosen people (Deut. 7:7–9). God chose Jacob's descendants as the ones he would call "my people" (Isa. 40:1). Most significantly, God set aside Israel as the one through whom the Messiah would enter the world and reign forever (Ps. 89:35–36). God shaped Israel in a wrestling match so that he might draw him intimately to his purposes. Israel became God's treasured possession (Exod. 19:5–6). Do you see the principle? The more God works on us, the deeper into possession we go. And the deeper into possession we go, the more we can see our purpose.

OUR SEARCH FOR MEANING

In his classic book *Man's Search for Meaning*, Viktor Frankl argued that humankind's greatest pursuit is to find the meaning of life.[1] To find purpose. Frankl, who was a Jewish psychiatrist, was put into concentration camps during WWII. Having lived at the extremes of society, from an elite social status to a prisoner, he was able to conclude that no matter the circumstances of life, humans want to know their meaning. In the concentration camps, those who found a purpose for living were more likely to survive the harsh conditions. Those who lost their purpose for living soon lost their ability to live—they succumbed to physical weakness, disease, and even death. Therefore, he said, it was imperative for him to help the other prisoners find their purpose. It was a matter of life or death.

In the book, Frankl turned the tables on our quest for meaning. He said that most people demand, "What is the purpose of my life?" However, Frankl suggested that the superior question to ask is "What is life asking of me right now?" Instead of demanding a purpose from your life, give your life purpose!

You might bristle at this idea, as if we can really give our lives meaning. After all, hasn't God given our lives meaning already? Isn't our purpose to glorify God and enjoy him forever, as the Westminster Shorter Catechism says?[2] While that is true, it doesn't tell us how to glorify and enjoy God. Frankl's insights push us to discern the Potter's hand in our daily lives. It might be helpful to reword Frankl's dictum as "What is *the Potter* asking of me right now?" or "What is the Potter forming me to do?" Discerning what the Potter is asking of us right now is the first step on the road to glorifying him. The second step, of course, is to obey.

What is life calling you to do right now? How are the things of life shaping you right now? What are they forming you to be? To do? Frankl's concern was that we figure out how to change ourselves in order to be the kinds of people who can respond with faith to the circumstances around us.

When I was in college, I redshirted my freshman year. This meant that to preserve another year of wrestling eligibility, I would not wrestle in any matches, but only practice. During the middle of the year, our

134-pounder broke his ribs. Coach decided to take away my redshirt status and have me wrestle in his place. Not only was he asking a fresh-man to wrestle, but also he was asking me to wrestle varsity. Oh yeah, and 134 wasn't my weight class; I was a 126-pounder. On top of this, he wanted me to wrestle in a meet against a top-notch wrestling school. My opponent would be a grappler who finished second in the nation the year before.

As I was going out onto the mat, heading into the lion's den, my coach grabbed me by the head and gave me a last-second pep talk. "Sam, just don't get pinned!" Instructions received, I went out and did my best to fulfill what he was calling me to do—and for the record, I did not get pinned.

Did you see what life was calling me to do in this admittedly trivial example? Life was calling me to stop redshirting, start wrestling varsity in a new weight class, face an opponent who was second in the nation, and avoid getting pinned. What was my purpose in that moment? My purpose was to do what life was calling me to do. That was what I was being shaped for: to go nobly into battle.

Extract the principle from this example and you can see what Frankl was saying. Life has a way of shaping us with its hands, putting us in situations and making demands of us, much like my coach did. Hear the question again: What is life demanding of you right now? What is the Coach calling you to do? Is he calling you to wrestle an opponent who outstrides you in every way? Is he calling you off the bench sooner than you expected? Is he calling you just to survive the best that you can? Is he calling you to set aside your desires? Face a fear? Make a sacrifice?

Once we grasp this principle, we can learn how to discover and retain our purpose, no matter how hard life spins us. If you're like me, you might think the purpose in your life is to change the situation you're in. Well, I have some liberating news for you: *it's not.* Your purpose is not to change the people and situations and demands of life—trust God to do that—your purpose is to rise to the occasion. Your purpose is to change yourself. Frankl concluded hauntingly:

> We must never forget that we may also find meaning in life even when confronted with a hopeless situation, when facing a fate that cannot be changed. For what then matters is to bear witness to the uniquely human potential at its best, which is to transform a personal tragedy into a triumph, to turn one's predicament into a human achievement. When we are no longer able to change a situation—just think of an incurable disease such as inoperable cancer—we are challenged to change ourselves.[3]

Our purpose is to change our tragedies into triumphs. How do we do this? By turning our predicaments into achievements. If you can't change your situation, then you can change yourself, with God's help. Face your challenge with dignity, character, boldness, and faith. Don't let your tragedy beat you down and cause you to give up, to become bitter, angry, faithless, hopeless, resentful, or envious. Use it as an opportunity to show the world the potential of what God has been shaping you to be.

There's a memorable scene in C. S. Lewis's *The Last Battle* when the eagle named Farsight brings devastating news to his companions. Farsight tells them that their mighty warrior, Roonwit the Centaur, has been struck with a mortal blow. The Eagle relays to his friends, "I was with him in his last hour and he gave me this message to your Majesty: to remember that all worlds draw to an end and that noble death is a treasure which no one is too poor to buy."[4] What a profound statement! As Roonwit lay dying, unable to change his circumstances in this most extreme of examples, he was able to change himself. He was able to meet tragedy head-on with faith, dying a "noble death."

This is what we're all called to do. In our last hour, will we be able to die a noble death? Will we die still believing in the goodness of God, still trusting that the Potter is in control, still upholding the cause of righteousness? Or will we give up, call it all a hoax, and betray that we never trusted God in the first place?

As Roonwit said, "no one is too poor to buy" this noblest of treasures. No matter your class, status, abilities, or inabilities, all it takes is your life. We may or may not like the way that the Potter has shaped us and what he is doing in our lives, but we can still respond in trust. We can still live a noble life and die a noble death. The alternative, as Roonwit intimated, is foolishness, for "all worlds draw to an end." Why do we live as if we will not die? As if tragedy and death are somehow a surprise? If we allow him, our gracious and wise Potter will form us to be the kinds of people who can face the inevitable with confidence and grace.

TO BE A BLESSING

There are two times in Genesis where God discussed Jacob's name change to Israel, chapters 32 and 35. In both chapters the name change is linked with "blessing." God would bless Israel and he would use Israel to be a blessing to the world, just as God earlier promised Abraham (Gen. 12:1–3). God was shaping his people to be the conduit of divine blessing to the world. And so it is with us. God is forming us to carry his blessing to those around us.

Louise was reminiscing about her grandchildren. She had a hard life, to say the least, and was marveling at the opportunities her grandchildren were experiencing. Thumbing through their school yearbook, she said to me, "I can't help but think how my life would have turned out if I had been given all of these opportunities." She was referring to her grandchildren's rigorous school, extracurricular activities, and positive friends. She had known none of these things growing up.

I looked at her and said, "Maybe you were not the one to be given the opportunity, but maybe you were the one *to give* the opportunity." Looking at her face and seeing the love she had for her grandchildren, I knew that she wouldn't change that for the world. Finding our purpose is better than having mere opportunities. God is forming us through all the trials and triumphs of life to be the kinds of people who will give blessing and opportunity to others.

That is our calling, which we strive to fulfill, born from a soul tattoo that reads "You are mine." When you discover this soul tattoo, you are poised to overcome the hardness of life, not by escaping it, but by truly entering it. Those who discover and embrace God's possession of them can face anything, because they know that he has been shaping them and he continues to shape them into extraordinary human beings who carry stains on their souls that no scars can erase.

CHAPTER 3

THE COST

But now thus says the LORD, he who created
you, O Jacob, he who formed you, O Israel:
"Fear not, for I have redeemed you; I have
called you by name, you are mine."

Isaiah 43:1

THE LION

Eric sat in Grant Park by a fountain with his wife and children. He held one of his kids in his rough hands, bouncing the little guy on his knee. I noticed his tattoo right away. It was a single-needle tattoo, a gorgeous sketch of a lion's head on the side of Eric's dark neck. He was very up front with its meaning, saying, "I am the man of my household, and I need to be strong for my family, just like a lion." I glanced at his wife; she didn't seem to have a problem with that. She bounced their other child on her knee.

But what if Eric, for whatever reason, lost his family? What if they were captured? Enslaved? Then what? Though I didn't ask him such a peculiar and hypothetical question, I'm fairly confident of what his response would be. He would assure me that he would go searching for them, do whatever it took to bring them home, pay whatever price needed to be paid. Eric, a strong young man from the

South Side of Chicago, seemed like that kind of guy. The lion on the outside betrayed the one within.

As we've been examining the tattoo "You are mine," we've learned that we belong to God by creation and by formation. We go even deeper now into God's intention behind this soul tattoo. We must consider redemption, which is the ultimate expression of our possession to God. God wants his people to know that they belong to him by redemption, especially when they're in the midst of exile. His claim on them is stronger than their captivity; his ink on their souls runs deeper than the scars on their skin.

Redemption is like a receipt. I am writing this chapter at my local coffee shop. Let's imagine that I bought one of the shop's new ceramic mugs and brought it to the table at which I am writing. Someone could see the new mug and accuse me of stealing it. But I could easily dismiss their accusation by producing the receipt. The receipt is proof that the mug is mine and that no more payment is needed. Likewise, redemption is proof that God's people belong to him and that nothing else needs to be done to ensure that they are secure. *They are secure.* They are his. When the accusations and threats start flying, we must not lose sight of this truth. God wants us to look at the receipt on our souls. By now, you should know what's written there in permanent ink: "You are mine."

THE LAYERS OF REDEMPTION

Redemption is a strong and beautiful word that has layers of meaning in the Bible.[1] However, its original primary use was not as a religious word, though it has come to be so. In ancient times, it was used predominantly in secular contexts. The word was often associated with slavery and the redemption of slaves. It's sort of like being in a computer store and hearing the word *apple*. You'll most likely think of the technology company first and maybe the fruit second. *Redemption* carries with it certain associations that are crucial to bear in mind if we're going to arrest its most exciting meaning.

In *The Apostolic Preaching of the Cross*, scholar Leon Morris started his discussion of *redemption* by examining its Greek roots. While Isaiah's book was originally written in Hebrew, it will help our discussion if we consider it through another language. The Greek verb *redeem* has its roots in the common verb *to loose*. To redeem is to loosen something so that it can be free. Think of loosening your laces and setting your foot free of your shoe. Or think of loosening an object from the grip of your hand. Redemption is to release something from the grip of another.

However, redemption is not just deliverance. There are more layers to it than that. If we don't consider these layers, we will miss the deeper truth of redemption and what a treasure it really is. Those layers are: captivity, slavery, price, family, and sacrifice.

CAPTIVITY

Redemption is not just deliverance but deliverance *from captivity*. That's an important distinction. If we don't know about our captivity, then we won't see the need to seek redemption. We'll just continue on mindlessly in the grip of our captor, not realizing there are better options for us. We'll settle down in this world as if there were no other.

God's people were in captivity in Babylon, away from their real home. Captivity is both dislocation and alienation. It's to be trapped in a foreign place. One of the goals of redemption is to bring us out of captivity so that we can return to where we truly belong. We'd be foolish to settle down in the place of our captivity, forgetting all about our true home.

When God says, "I will redeem you," he is at the same time reminding us that we are in captivity. He is telling us that we are out of place *and* that there is a better place. I know it might be hard to believe that today we are in captivity, but remember, for redemption to make sense, we must pull its layers over us like blankets. Tim Keller presented a compelling analogy to support this point. Just think of a fish out of water—can it survive? Of course not. Think of a human being in outer space—can he survive without special equipment? Of course not. His point was that living things can't survive when they are outside of their natural environments, the homes for which they were made.[2]

As we all know, humans die. We don't survive. Have you ever thought why? One reason is that we are not in our natural environment. We were made for another kind of world. "But," someone might retort, "humans do survive! In fact they can live to be a hundred years old!" Granted, a hundred years is a long time for a human to live. But if you compare one hundred years to one hundred billion years, it's not that long at all. What if you compare one hundred years to one hundred billion centuries? One hundred billion eons? One hundred trillion eons? You get the idea. Humans live for only a few pathetic breaths. Or, as Scripture puts it, "What is your life? For you are a mist that appears for a little time and then vanishes" (James

4:14). In the infinite scheme of things, our lives are a mist, which will be gone by sunrise. We are definitely not at home in this present world; we must have been made for another. Redemption assumes that we're perishing in captivity. We are in exile from our true home.

SLAVERY

Redemption isn't just deliverance, and it's not just deliverance from captivity; it's deliverance from captivity as *slaves*. This is the second layer of meaning that we must take to heart. We are slaves, no matter how dreadful or humiliating that might sound. We serve the desires of malevolent masters. There are plenty of instances of slavery in the Bible, such as when the Israelites were slaves in Egypt. And there are plenty of real-life examples of slavery today, each of them heartbreaking in every way. But whether or not we are slaves in the obvious understanding, we are all slaves according to the spiritual meaning.

As slaves, we are not free to follow our own wishes, but only the demands of our masters. We have no rights; we must obey. In spiritual terms, our masters are sin and death. We are just as much captives to sin and death as Israel was to Egypt. Simply stated, sin is loving and obeying other things more than you love and obey God. And since God is the Center and Giver of life, to submit to a new master is equivalent to rushing headlong into death. The one who sins chooses to cut herself off from the Source of life, reaping the devastating result: death. Scripture describes it this way: "The wages of sin is death" (Rom. 6:23).

You and I inherited a sin nature as much as we inherited a human nature. There was nothing we could do about it; we were born into slavery. Even so, every day we prove our eligibility to be slaves by the fact that we actively sin, both physically and mentally. There is no way (apart from God's grace) to escape either the power of sin or the presence of sin. There is also no way to escape the fruit of sin, which is death. Our lives are on course to die, and we can't do anything to stop it. Better health won't stop it, more wealth won't stop it, not even greater religious devotion will stop it. In one way, we are basically born dead. We are born in death's grip, and it is only a matter of time before we are crushed by it.

Someone once asked me, "If Jesus died for us, then why do we still have to die?" This is a very important question. I told him the story of Odysseus and Polyphemus, that hideous Cyclops who captured Odysseus and his men inside his cave. Slowly, the grotesque giant began to bash the Greeks against the stone floor and munch them like apples. The Greeks were unable to escape from Polyphemus or his cave. They were completely trapped and hopeless.

But one day, Odysseus devised a plan. When Polyphemus returned after a long day's work, Odysseus gave him some robust wine. Once the giant was drunk and passed out in the cave, Odysseus sharpened a long piece of timber, completing the job by heating its end like a red-hot poker. With all his strength, he buried it into the Cyclops's eye, blinding him. In the commotion that ensued, the Greeks were able to conceal themselves beneath some sheep and escape the cave unseen. Without a heroic deliverer, they would have succumbed to a terrible fate.

It is as if we were all born inside the cave. My friend's question assumed that we were born alive, outside the cave. If that were the case, then his confusion would be warranted. But what if we were actually born inside the cave? What if we were born in the grip of death? Then the question changes from "Why do we still have to die?" to "How are we going to escape from the cave?" That's the real question. How are you and I going to escape from the rotten grave, from the iron grip of sin and death? We were not born into the place where we truly belong; we were born into captivity, at the hungry feet of Polyphemus. Only when we understand our birth into slavery can we see the meaning of Jesus's death. Jesus did not die to redeem living people, but dead ones.

This causes me to rethink my definition of freedom. True freedom is not the granting of more rights, nor is it having more privileges, per se. Neither rights nor privileges matter so long as I wake up every morning under the watchful eye of a Cyclops. More of this or more of that won't bring about significant changes if at the end of the day I am still swallowed up. True freedom is being free of the Cyclops and the cave. True freedom is being redeemed from sin and death.

PRICE

This brings us to a third layer of meaning for redemption. Redemption isn't free—it comes with a cost. "The basic idea in redemption is the paying of a ransom price to secure a liberation."[3] The whole mechanism of redemption depends on the payment of a price. Like a mousetrap, whose parts are "irreducibly complex"[4] in that without one part the whole will not function, so redemption will fail if payment is not given. Nothing will be "loosed" if payment isn't placed on the eager catch; sinners will not be sprung from captivity. Redemption is deliverance *by payment of a price.*

It's crucial that we understand this. If you're looking for freedom, then you can't find it apart from someone who is willing to pay the price. Are you hung up on a sin? Are you stuck in a paralyzing behavior? Are you enslaved to certain appetites and addictions? Are you beginning to get hopeless? Are you unsure how you'll ever be set free? *There is no deliverance without payment.*

Some people take the ideals of Christianity and try to twist them into something they are not. They style Jesus into certain liberation theologies or cultural agendas. They want the ethical teachings of Jesus, but they don't want the payment that Jesus gave, as if this payment would keep them trapped in the barbarism of the past rather than catapult them into the future. But Christianity refuses to comply because there is no liberation apart from the payment that was given for our redemption. You can't take the icing and leave the cake. Freedom begins where slavery ends; slavery ends when the ransom price is paid by a Hero who is willing to make the sacrifice for those he loves.

Somebody has to pay for sin, either us or God. Forgiveness is not without cost. What word do you notice in for*give*ness? To forgive someone means to give a gift that he or she needs but does not deserve. If I knock a hole in your television, you might be very kind to me and forgive me, but that doesn't fix the problem.[5] There is still a hole in your television, and someone has to pay for it. You can be fair and make me pay for it—after all, I'm the one who put the hole there. Or you can grant forgiveness and give me a gift that I don't deserve by paying for it yourself, freeing me from my debt.

When it comes to our sins, God could be fair and make us pay for them. Or he could grant forgiveness and give us a gift that we don't deserve. This is redemption: to give the gift that releases a prisoner from debt.

FAMILY

Why would you give a gift like this? Why would God give us a gift like this? In the Hebrew, there are three main words for *redeem*. The one used in Isaiah 43:1 is *ga'al*, which has specific and compelling overtones that the others do not. *Ga'al* suggests an added sense of family obligation or duty, giving it a tender and compassionate nuance. Keep in mind that redemption itself often deals with things that once were ours but now we have lost. Having lost that which we loved, we will do whatever it takes, pay whatever is owed, to get it back. We'll be a lion if we have to.

We can get a better understanding of this important concept by studying places where *ga'al* is used in the Bible. One of the best examples is found in the book of Ruth. Boaz was a kinsman redeemer to Ruth. When he found out that Ruth's husband had died, it was up to him to redeem her. She was lost on multiple levels and would absolutely struggle to survive if he didn't step forward to redeem her. Not only did he save her, but also he brought her into his family. Can you see the tender side to *ga'al*?

Or consider a case where someone is forced to go into slavery in order to pay off a debt. In ancient times, this was how debt was typically settled. The only other way out would be through the payment of a ransom. According to Leviticus 25:48–49, a family member could redeem the person in debt. Once redeemed, that person would be welcomed back into the family. You can imagine the day when the ransom was paid and the family welcomed him home with open arms!

Finally, let's look at a fascinating, albeit extreme case in Numbers 35. Put yourself in ancient times and imagine that one of your family members unintentionally killed another person. Perhaps it was a farming accident—keep in mind the precariousness of ancient times. God directed his people to establish "cities of refuge" as safe places for people such as your family member to live.

But let's say someone purposefully killed one of your family members, striking your relative with iron, wood, or stone. Such a murderer could not find a city of refuge. Instead, God instructed his people to find an "avenger of blood" (a *ga'al*) to strike down the murderer (Num. 35:19). This was the ultimate kinsman redeemer. He made the murderer "pay the price" for what he did to your family. Family devotion plays an important role in the meaning of the word *ga'al*. Redemption carries with it the strong desire to fight for one's family.

Rounding out our look at *ga'al*, it's interesting to see that Isaiah often used this word in chapters 40–66; in fact, he used it thirteen times, which is a lot compared with the rest of Scripture. Gazing upon the text of Isaiah 40–66 is like standing in a family room surrounded by people who love you and will fight for you. That's the feel God wants to communicate to us about redemption. Redemption is deliverance from captivity as slaves through the payment of a price, in order to restore to the family that which was lost.

SACRIFICE

We come now to the final layer. If we were discussing redemption strictly from a human vantage point, our definition would be complete. However, our concern is with ultimate redemption. Godly redemption. We want to know what God meant in Isaiah 43:1 when he said, "Fear not, for I have redeemed you." God alone stands behind that pronoun "I."

When a human redeems something, he or she makes payment to another human. But this is unthinkable when it comes to God. When God is the subject of the verb *redeem*, he does not make any payments to humans. What kind of a God would he be if he owed anything to mortals? Scripture never portrays God making a payment to humans.

So how is God going to redeem us from our captors if he is unable to make a payment to them for us? Here's how Scripture answers that question:

> I am the LORD, and I will bring you out from under
> the burdens of the Egyptians, and I will deliver you
> from slavery to them, and I will redeem you with an
> outstretched arm and with great acts of judgment.
> I will take you to be my people, and I will be your
> God, and you shall know that I am the LORD your
> God, who has brought you out from under the
> burdens of the Egyptians. (Exod. 6:6–7)

Notice that God did not say, "I will pay the ransom price that is owed *to the Egyptians* for you." God's economy does not consist of putting himself in debt to others. Instead, God said that he would redeem his people "with an outstretched arm and with great acts of judgment." These terms describe the vigorous sacrifice God is willing to make for his people.

All redemption entails sacrifice; however, when God makes a sacrifice, it is at the expense of himself. He doesn't make humans pay; instead, he absorbs the cost for redemption within his own being. In addition, he does not give this payment to humans. He gives it to himself. God's loving sacrifice is the only way in which humans can be free. But how can this be? What kind of a God is able both to make a ransom *and* to receive a ransom?

THE ELEGANT DIALOGUE

We come now to the most inviolable source of our security, which is anchored within the very being of God. This is where we can feel the ink of "You are mine" touching our souls. We must go into God's council room and discover the contract he made with himself. As Martyn Lloyd-Jones wrote, "God purposed and planned a great way of redemption." He added provocatively, "Redemption is a greater work even than creation."[6] God's work in creation was breathtaking and God's work in formation is gripping, but God's work of redemption is his greatest. The Father made a contract with his Son for our redemption, not as an afterthought, but as his original strategy. The plan to save sinners was "the greatest affair, between persons of the highest sovereignty and majesty, that ever was transacted either in heaven or earth, or ever will be."[7]

Thomas Goodwin referred to the conversation in Isaiah 49:1–7 as the most "Elegant Dialogue."[8] This is a beautiful portrayal of a conversation God the Father had with God the Son about saving people from their sins. Just one chapter before, God made it clear that his people needed to be redeemed from their sins. God lamented, "Oh that you had paid attention to my commandments! Then your peace would have been like a river" (Isa. 48:18). Instead, God had to make this assessment of his people: "There is no peace … for the wicked!" (v. 22). Because of this, death was coming to his people, and there was no city of refuge for them, unless an ultimate kinsman redeemer could step forward.

This is the backdrop of the Elegant Dialogue in Isaiah 49:1–7: Israel needed to be redeemed, but there was no one worthy enough to do it. In fact, Israel herself was supposed to be the redeemer of the world, but she had failed miserably. That's when God's Servant stepped forward and said:

> The LORD called me from the womb,
>> from the body of my mother he named my
>> name.
> He made my mouth like a sharp sword;
>> in the shadow of his hand he hid me;
> he made me a polished arrow;
>> in his quiver he hid me away. (Isa. 49:1–2)

The Servant was the Messiah of Israel, the very Son of God. We are told that he would be born of a human mother and sent as an arrow from God. He would be both fully human and fully God. His mission was described next: "And he said to me, 'You are my servant, Israel, in whom I will be glorified'" (Isa. 49:3).

Notice that he named the Servant "Israel." Since the nation of Israel had failed at being faithful to God, God's plan was to send his Son as the true Israel who would not fail at keeping his commands and walking in his ways. God sent his Son to redeem the nation of Israel, and his Son agreed (Isa. 49:5). However, the Son was not satisfied with merely redeeming the people of Israel; he wanted to redeem more! Just to redeem Israel was "too light a thing" (v. 6). In response, as the Elegant Dialogue continued, the Father said to his Servant: "I will make you as a light for the nations, that my salvation may reach to the end of the earth" (v. 6).

The contract between the Father and the Son states that the Son will be the Redeemer (*ga'al*) of the whole world, not just the nation of Israel. He will be the ultimate Kinsman Redeemer who performs his duty lovingly and faithfully when all the other redeemers fail.

JESUS

This brings us to the amazing person of Jesus Christ, a participant in the Elegant Dialogue, the ultimate Kinsman Redeemer, and the incarnate expression of God's love for us. Here's what Scripture says about him:

> For God so loved the world, that he gave his only Son, that whoever believes in him should not perish but have eternal life. For God did not send his Son into the world to condemn the world, but in order that the world might be saved through him. (John 3:16–17)

God sent his Son to be our Redeemer, allowing God the ability both to pay for our sins and to receive payment for our sins. It is his work from beginning to end. This means that our security is perfect, for nothing can corrupt the contract that he made with himself to secure our salvation. In other words, "You are mine!"

NEW WORTH

Equations, by definition, have to be equal on both sides of the equal sign. If the left side of the equation works out to be forty-two, then the right side must also work out to be forty-two. Well, purchases are like that too. They have to be equal on both sides. If you are selling a car for $5,000, then I had better give you $5,000 for it. If not, then I still owe you.

Let's say that I want to buy a handbag from someone. The seller asks $25 for it, so that's the amount I pay. What is the bag worth? That's right, it's worth $25. Now, let's say that I *really* want your handbag. Because I want it so badly, I give you $50,000 for it. I know that's an unrealistic and absurd amount, but just hear me out. Now how much is the handbag worth? If you say $25, you're wrong. If I give you $50,000 for your handbag, then it's now worth $50,000. And nobody had better try to steal it from me! It's worth way too much!

Jesus is priceless. But how much are *you* worth? Because God gave his only Son for you, you're wrong if you think you're worth only about as much as a $25 handbag. The priceless value of the Son of God doesn't just vanish into thin air; it lands right on your head. You are now worth that much to him.

Where does your worth come from? It comes from the cross of Jesus Christ, who was given as the payment of ransom for our sins to release us from the terrible jaws of sin and death. We have a blood-bought worth.

God says to us, "Fear not, for I have redeemed you." Can you see now why God says, "Fear not"? Are you afraid that you're worthless? Are you afraid that nobody wants you? Are you afraid that God won't be there for you? Are you afraid that God won't make good on his promises? Are you afraid that God has left you? Are you afraid that you've gone too far, sinned too much, or done too little? The Lord says to us, "*Fear not*, for I have redeemed you." God has paid for you to be free, truly free. He has tattooed on your soul "You are mine," which is the receipt of his massive love for you.

> What then shall we say to these things? If God is for us, who can be against us? He who did not spare his own Son but gave him up for us all, how will he not also with him graciously give us all things? (Rom. 8:31–32)

CHAPTER 4

YOUR APPOINTMENT

But now thus says the LORD, he who created you, O Jacob,
he who formed you, O Israel: "Fear not, for I have redeemed
you; I have called you by name, you are mine."

Isaiah 43:1

A THIRD KIND OF PERSON

So far we have seen that we belong to God by *creation, formation,* and *redemption.* Now let's look at how we belong to God by *invitation.* Before we begin, it's worth reflecting on the amazing first verse of Isaiah 43. Have you ever known such treasure? These are the kinds of riches our hearts have always longed for but have never been able to find: God created us because he wanted us; God forms us so that he can possess us; God redeemed us to bring us back home to where we belong. This verse displays the strong action of God, working for his people. The final part of the verse reads, "I have called you by name." God's calling makes our response possible. It gives us hope.

I want to start this chapter by mentioning a third kind of person. This person has known something of Jesus but still can't see clearly. The story of the blind man in Mark 8:22–26 tells us about

this kind of person: Some people brought a blind man to Jesus and
begged their Lord to touch him. Jesus did what they asked. He laid
his hands on the man's eyes and healed him—sort of. "Do you see
anything?" Jesus asked the man. The man responded, "I see people,
but they look like trees, walking." In response, Jesus laid his hands
on the man a second time. When the man opened his eyes, his sight
was completely restored, "and he saw everything clearly." The strange
part about this miracle is that it took Jesus two tries, at least that's
what it looks like on the surface. The truth, however, is that Jesus
could heal blindness on just one attempt; in fact, just two chapters
later, Jesus healed Bartimaeus instantly (Mark 10:46–52). So it's not
as if Jesus swung, missed, and then took another swing at the ball.
Jesus healed the man in degrees to teach his followers a lesson about
the steps involved in spiritual sight.

In the Bible, blindness is often a metaphor for a lack of spiritual perception. In this world, there are those who are blind to God
and those who are not—two kinds of people. But Jesus has a much
more nuanced view of the human condition, which makes room for
another kind of person. He doesn't restrict people to rigid categories
but recognizes where they are in order to invite them a step closer to
him. That's what he was doing with the blind man. Religion likes to
warn, "You are either a saint or a sinner!" But Jesus is more patient
and realistic.

After one touch from Jesus, the blind man was no longer blind,
but he still could not see. Yes, he could see *something*, but his sight
wasn't how it should've been. If I tell you that in my sight humans look
like trees and trees look like elephants, then you should be concerned!
"Yes, I can see, but I can't see clearly!" On one level, not being able

to see clearly is the same as not seeing at all. I learned this in Little League baseball when my coach discovered that I needed glasses. I'm not blind, but I still can't see. I am the third kind of person. What am I to do? I need Jesus to bring me to the next level of sight.

Many of us fall into this third category. On the one hand, we know that this world is messed up and life is not how it should be. On the other hand, we don't know what the answer is and we can't fix the problem ourselves. Many people know that there is a God, but they don't know who he is. They know that the answers to life's problems can't be found in things such as better politics or more education, but they don't know where else to look. They know something is wrong in their lives, but they don't know how to make it right. Perhaps you know that God created you and is forming you. Maybe you've heard the story of how God redeemed you. But still you don't quite get what that means. You were healed of one kind of blindness but not the other.

Just like the blind man, we need to admit that we can't see clearly. We need to beg Jesus to touch us a second time. Maybe you know that God is capable of spiritual healing, but you have not yet experienced this sort of thing for yourself. You know that he offers redemption, but you don't know if you are redeemed. You know about forgiveness, but you don't know if such amazing grace is for you. In this chapter, we'll learn that God calls us by name. He gives us a personal invitation to receive his salvation. He wants us to see clearly. *"I have called you by name, you are mine."*

Have you heard God's invitation? God wants you to hear his call and respond in faith. There are four aspects to this call: inspiration, invitation, inversion, and identification.

INSPIRATION

I was always told that you weren't supposed to look at a solar eclipse because it could cause blindness. Whatever the damage a solar eclipse might do to your eyes, it's an appropriate way through which to view Isaiah's strategy for vouchsafing inspiration in his book. Remember Isaiah's theme "Though God's people fail, God's Servant will prevail"? His entire book is a showcase for God's Servant, the Savior. That's what Isaiah wanted the people to see, even as their lives had been eclipsed by the terrible trials of Babylon. But who is this Savior? Throughout the book, Isaiah revealed the Messiah, who is the better King, the more faithful Servant, and the more trustworthy Conqueror. Yes, there are trials, and we are to see the trials, but there is also hope, which we are also meant to see. This is where the metaphor of the eclipse comes into play.

A solar eclipse occurs when the moon moves between the earth and the sun, smearing the sun's light with a thick smudge—at least that's how it looks from earth's vantage point. Isaiah saw a similar vision from his own limited vantage point, as he looked across the expanse of world history. It was as if he had seen three solar eclipses. In each eclipse, the Savior was the bright sun, shining out from behind a temporary obstacle. The temporary obstacles were the events of world history, which threatened to darken our hope. The first eclipse was the failure of King Ahaz. The second was the failure of King Hezekiah's faith. The third was the Babylonian captivity. Each of these was a "moon," a dark spot on the horizon blocking the sun. That's what our trials are like. It's easy to see just the dark spots because they are so prominent, while hope is harder to find.

But Isaiah didn't see just the dark spots. In each instance, he got a vision of the Savior, like a sun behind our trials, surrounding them with the piercing glow of promise. J. Alec Motyer outlined these three sections of Isaiah's book and the role of the Savior in each: the glorious King yet to come (chapters 1–37); the Servant of the Lord (chapters 38–55); and the coming Conqueror (chapters 56–66).[1] In each section there is a dark spot and then a shining solution. There is human failure and divine rescue. It's worth reading through the verses in Isaiah's book that refer to the Savior.[2] He shines out as our hope from behind the trials of life. The presence of his glow is meant to inspire us to keep pressing forward, for the trials of this life are just as passing as a moon during a solar eclipse. Trials may blur or momentarily obscure our vision, but we are still able to see something of the Savior.

INVITATION

We belong to God by invitation. As we read through the Bible and learn about the glowing hope of our Savior, we hear his invitation to follow him. When we read God's words in Isaiah 43:1, "I have called you by name," we realize that his call demands a response. The word for "call" means to invite, summon, or proclaim. A colloquial definition might be "Hey, you! Come here!" When God calls us, he wants us to *perceive* him and he wants us to *respond* to him.

When God called to Adam and Eve in the garden of Eden, he said, "Where are you?" (Gen. 3:9). God wanted them to know that he was looking for them, *and* God wanted them to respond to him. To call someone is to initiate a relationship and to invite a response.

One time when I was a little boy, I got lost in an amusement park. I frantically searched for my parents for what seemed like ages. How did I find them? I heard their voices calling my name. Because they called me, I knew where to go. They called and I answered, and the relationship was able to move forward.

Every call needs a response. God's call can be found in the pages of the Bible, which is his word to us. God calls us through heartrending poetry, practical wisdom, and terrifying prophecy. He calls us through compelling narrative, engaging history, and inspiring letters. He calls us through logic, hyperbole, proverb, salutation, doxology, song, prediction, vision, parable, diary, complaint, praise, lament, prayer, warning, and encouragement. God calls us in innumerable ways. But do we respond in faith?

When I get busy, I tend not to respond to people when they try to contact me. They'll use email, texting, Facebook, Twitter, instant messaging, and so forth. When I'm busy, I ignore all these forms of communication, except when the person trying to reach me is my wife. Whenever her name lights up on my phone, I answer. Her call, like every call, demands a response; however, her call, *unlike* every other call, is special. How much more special is God's call to us? He is the one who created us, is forming us, and has redeemed us. It's not just anyone who's calling our names; it's God, our hearts' greatest desire, the one to whom we owe our lives.

INVERSION

Now we come to a really wonderful part of this story, one that's as surprising as an ample check in the mail. The shock is due to our expectations. We expect God to behave one way, but as it turns out, he can behave in any way he wants. Religion has trained us to expect a certain order to things, and so has daily living for that matter. According to most world religions, our response to God comes before our salvation. They teach that we accumulate a certain number of achievements throughout life that are measured against God's criteria. If we don't measure up, we don't earn salvation. But if we do measure up, then God will reward us accordingly.

Islam teaches that if you are obedient, you will be rewarded with eternal life. Obedience is defined by things such as fasting, praying, pilgrimage, charity, and saying a particular creed. If you respond to God's call the right way, you'll be saved. According to Hinduism, the only way out of the vicious cycle of life is to realize your oneness with the universe. When you finally manage to realize this and merge with the universe, then you can be freed. Buddhism teaches that we're trapped in a cycle and that release can be found only through the elimination of desire and through the Eightfold Path. How you follow the call determines your fate; human effort comes before divine salvation.

But the God of the Bible is not like any other god. He inverts calling and redemption. To invert is to put something upside down, out of order, in a way that you wouldn't expect and that goes against the norm. Notice the inversion in Isaiah 43:1. Can you spot it? Read the verse again: "But now thus says the LORD, he who created you, O Jacob, he who formed you, O Israel: 'Fear not, for I have redeemed you; I have called you by name, you are mine.'"

There is a great inversion here, which takes the careful reader by surprise. To help you see it, consider a common objection I get from my non-Christian friends when I invite them to church. They usually say something like "I can't go to church because I'd be struck dead!" or "God won't listen to my prayers because I'm so bad." What's the assumption behind these kinds of statements? The same assumption found in most world religions: you have to get your life in order before you try to get into God's presence. The thought is that before God will accept you, you have to straighten out your life. The belief is that effort comes before salvation, calling before redemption.

God's calling is different, radically different. *God puts salvation before invitation.* The order of these ideas in Isaiah 43:1 is crucial to grasp. God redeems us before he calls us to himself. Can you imagine if Hinduism stated that we're released from the cycle of life before we have to try? Can you imagine if Islam taught that Allah rewarded us with eternal life before we have to be obedient to him? These religions don't teach those ways because they are intrinsically works based. You have to earn your keep. Of course, it isn't surprising why so many people fall easily into believing this is how God must work. Our daily lives are substantively works based. Can you imagine your boss giving you a paycheck before you ever clocked in? Can you imagine your teacher giving you an A+ before you did any of the assignments? Can you imagine your coach making you captain of the team before you were on it? Can you imagine getting first chair in the orchestra before you learned to play the violin? That kind of thinking goes against our understanding of real life. And it's why God's great inversion is both surprising and powerful. "Fear not, for I have *redeemed* you; I have *called* you by name." *God provides us with redemption before he asks us to respond to his calling.*

The same was true for the ancient Israelites. Think about their redemption from Egypt and the giving of the law. Which came first, invitation or redemption? God sent the plagues and saved his people from the awful clutches of Pharaoh (Exod. 14) *before* he gave them the law on Mount Sinai (Exod. 20). Once they were redeemed, then he invited them to live holy lives according to the Ten Commandments and the rest of the law. The God of the Bible places redemption before invitation. He invites us to respond to him only after he saves us.

And here's a critical point—don't miss this—our salvation does not depend on our performance, how well we uphold the call. This may be harder to accept than God's inversion because our lives are filled with performance-driven expectations. We grow weary from not living up to the expectations of others. This causes us to lose sight of hope. But God redeems us, so that we do not have to fear, and then he invites us to respond to him in faith. I remember talking with a Muslim student at Ohio State University. I asked him if he thought God would accept him into eternal life. I'll never forget the way that he paused, gave an uneasy smile, and said, "I hope so, but I'll never know for sure." Because of this, he was driven to earn his salvation through countless acts of obedience. He would never know if he had been good enough to earn God's salvation.

We are saved by grace and not by our performance (Eph. 2:8). God has redeemed us through the sacrifice of his Son on the cross. Freedom begins at the cross. Once we trust Jesus to redeem us, then we are called to follow him in obedience. The point is that everything is in place, and your soul is cleared. The door is open, and you need only to walk through it. The chair is open, and your appointment is paid for. The path is clear, and nothing is standing in your way; none of your sins can keep you from being entirely and eternally redeemed right now.

To be clear, I am not saying that everyone is given salvation automatically. I am saying that God redeems his children before he calls them to obedience. Obedience comes from faith in our ultimate Kinsman Redeemer, Jesus Christ.[3] The good news of the Bible is this great inversion. God only calls us to that which he has already made possible.

IDENTIFICATION

God said, "I have called you by name." What do you call yourself by? Do you call yourself by your accomplishments? If so, that's how you identify yourself. God does not call us by our accomplishments. Nor does God call us by our race or ethnicity, nor by our jobs or titles. He doesn't call us by our successes or failures, our status or our position. He calls us by name. You might even have a dream for your life, the kind of person you would like to be or the kind of future you would like to see. God doesn't call us by our dreams or desires either. He doesn't call us by our plans. It doesn't matter what you want to be; it matters what God has called you to be. He calls us by name.

Who are you? If God could know only one thing about you, what would you like him to know? That you were a good parent? An accomplished person? A community activist? Which "name" do you want to submit to God for his examination? When God says, "I have called you by name," he also provides the name! He doesn't name us according to our desires; rather, he names us according to his purposes for us. God names us according to *his* desires, accomplishments, and dreams.

We find these names in the book of Isaiah. We already learned how God changed Jacob's name to Israel. According to Isaiah 62:12, God has four new names for us too—names that might take us by surprise but are indicative of his holy character. God first calls us "The Holy People." Then he calls us "The Redeemed of the LORD." He also calls us "Sought Out" and "A City Not Forsaken." Notice that God calls us names that reflect his actions in our lives. His redemption has made us "The Holy People." His mighty sacrifice has made us "The Redeemed of the LORD." His relentless pursuit of us has made us "Sought Out." His perseverance with us has made us "A City Not Forsaken." Our identity flows from his. We are made in his image, and we are saved according to his ways.

You will never know who you are until you know who God is. The only way to find yourself is by pursuing God, learning about him, and making him the center of your existence. Until you do that, you'll remain spinning out of control, unable to find rest or satisfaction. Only when you pursue the one who created you, formed you, redeemed you, and is calling you can you discover who you truly are. To do anything else is to remain trapped in a myopic version of yourself, never discovering your true greatness. Your names are so much bolder than you could ever dream your accomplishments to be, for you are "The Holy People." You are more powerful than you could ever fathom, for you are "The Redeemed of the LORD." You are lovelier than you could ever imagine your appearance to be, for you are "Sought Out." You are more secure than you could ever think possible, for you are "A City Not Forsaken."

We need to stop listening to what others are calling us and embrace what God is calling us. Our identities do not rest in the accusations or flattery of others but in the sovereign love of God. It's his verdict that counts. Your name is not "Reject" but "Sought Out." Can you remind yourself of this? It will take some effort. But to ignore God is the equivalent to basing your life on a foundation of lies. The Bible contains the truths about who we are that will set us free from the lies that seek to limit us.

The negative names that others have called us are like coffee stains on our souls. They are like blotches on the sun. We don't know what to do with them, so we end up believing them. They've become a part of us, soaking into our identities. We believe these lies more than we believe the truth. I don't just want your blindness to be cured; I want you to see clearly. I want you to see clearly the way God has identified you. I want you to see that these names are a key to hope.

KEYS TO HOPE

The pilgrim named Christian and his friend were captured by a giant named Despair. Giant Despair threw them into his dark and stinking dungeon. They weren't allowed to have bread, water, or visitors. Giant Despair beat them mercilessly every day. The two pilgrims filled their days with groaning, lamentation, and regret. But still they didn't give up hope. Seeing their steadfastness, Giant Despair doubled his efforts, for his goal was for them to take their own lives. He even provided them with a noose, a knife, and a bottle of poison. Soon the two friends began to argue with each other about whether to use these devices of death. Surely death would be better than to endure such a miserable life. But Hopeful, the name of the other pilgrim, said, "Not everything is in the hands of the Giant Despair."

Seeing that the pilgrims still didn't give up and take their lives, Giant Despair took them to the castle yard, which was filled with the rotting bones of all the other pilgrims who had given up hope. At the sight of all these bones, Christian swooned, for he was hungry, bruised, and hopeless. But just when he was about to give up, he remembered that he had a key in his pocket, which was called Promise. He wondered if it would fit the locks that held them captive. Later in the story, as it turns out, the keys would work.

In the meantime, both the Giant and his wife couldn't figure out why the two pilgrims hadn't yet given up hope after all the beatings, starvation, and hideous sights. She woke up in the middle of the night with a terrible thought. Rousing her husband, she gasped to Giant Despair, "Perhaps they have pick-locks with them. That's why they live in hope."[4]

I have found this passing thought from a fictional character in *The Pilgrim's Progress* to be a perfect summary of what it means to be a Christian. Christians are those who "have pick-locks with them." Wherever they go, whether good or bad, they carry with them the keys of hope. When you're deep in the dungeon, you can reach in your pocket for a key of hope. When your sky is growing dark, a key of hope is at your fingertips. What are these keys? What are these pick-locks? Though they could be many things in the Christian life, I'd like to suggest that they are the names that God has given us.

"The Holy People" is a pick-lock. Use it to get out of doubt. "The Redeemed of the LORD" is a pick-lock. Use it to get out of fear. "Sought Out" is a pick-lock. Use it to get out of loneliness. "A City Not Forsaken" is a pick-lock. Use it to get out of despair. All of these keys are on a key ring, which is called "You are mine."

TATTOO 2

I WILL BE
WITH YOU

CHAPTER 5

IT WON'T BE TOO MUCH FOR YOU TO HANDLE

When you pass through the waters, I will be with you; and through the rivers, they shall not overwhelm you; when you walk through fire you shall not be burned, and the flame shall not consume you.

Isaiah 43:2

FIDELITY

It's one thing to know where we belong, but it's another thing to experience the one to whom we belong. This second soul tattoo is the practical working out of the first: "You are mine" leads to "I will be with you." We learned how God laid claim on our souls through creation, formation, redemption, and invitation. Now we see what this looks like in real life. Will God come through on his promises? Will he be there for us when we need him the most? One of the Hebrew names for God is "Lord." Roughly translated, "Lord" means "he who is." In other words, the very name of God means something like "he is the one who is always with you." He just is. He is present. *"I will be with you."*

At the heart of God's name is the claim of fidelity.

When I hear the word *fidelity*, I think of mothers. I'm aware this isn't a perfect correlation—there are good and bad mothers. But consider the good ones. They support their children. And when they can't be there for their kids, they long to be. I have seen this in my wife over and over again. Like many mothers, she not only has a tender desire to show affection to our children, but she also has a relentless drive to defend and care for them. Her intuition, level of concern, and capacity for them exceed my own. There are depths to her being as a mother that I can't even begin to understand or appreciate. She is a living, breathing definition of fidelity.

As I've been talking to people about their tattoos, I've been struck by how many of them symbolized the mother-child relationship. Many moms get tattoos that remind them of their children. These moms never want to lose sight of their children, even to the point of recording their presence permanently on their skin. I've also seen plenty of tattoos honoring moms. Debbie, whom I met in Chicago, has one such tattoo. She told me, "My mom passed away, and I got this tattoo for her. She was the only person in this world who understood me without words."

Though perhaps exemplified best by moms, our search for fidelity is not satisfied completely by them. Consider this verse from Isaiah: "Can a woman forget her nursing child, that she should have no compassion on the son of her womb? Even these may forget, yet I will not forget you" (Isa. 49:15).

A nursing mother will not forget about her child. How could she? She loves the child, and the child depends on her. Her heart is greatly stirred by the child, who came from her body, the very "son of her womb." Just as he came from the core of her being, so does she cleave to him with the same intensity, as if she were caring for a part of herself. However, even greater than her love for the child is God's abidance with us. Even when a mother is worn out, God will never fail us.

Tattooed on your soul is the mark of God's fidelity. *"I will be with you."* Long after our moms have failed us, God will still be there for us. The second verse of Isaiah 43 teaches us ten truths about God's fidelity.

TRUTH 1: YOU WILL GO THROUGH TRIALS

The first truth that we learn is that trials are inevitable. The verse does not say, *"If* you pass through the waters"; it says, *"When* you pass through the waters" and *"When* you walk through fire." Trials will happen, no matter how good or bad you live. God anticipates trials happening to you. They are on his calendar, so they do not surprise him. God is not waiting to see how you live today in order to determine whether to reward you or curse you tomorrow. That's not how trials work for God's children.

Trials are inevitable, but they are not synonymous with punishment. Punishment is what God did to his Son, Jesus, on the cross, as we learned in chapter 3. So bad was his punishment that it drove him to death and hell, on our behalf. Jesus absorbed the full punishment of God so that there is none left for us. God does not punish those of us who take shelter beneath the wings of Christ. However, we still have to walk through trials.

To live as if you're "above" trials is to live in denial of a fundamental part of what it means to be human in this fallen world. To
be a human is to be sinful. We must own that truth about ourselves
and, by doing so, move away from the absurd ways we cope with life.
The 1991 movie *What about Bob?* provides an interesting contrast
between two characters, one who embraces his creatureliness and
the other who doesn't. Bob, played by Bill Murray, has obsessive-
compulsive disorder because of his great fear of death. He's afraid
that his heart will one day stop beating or—in his words—his blad-
der will explode. Since he's so afraid of death, he copes with it by
trying to control (and clean) everything.

He eventually seeks help from a psychiatrist named Dr. Leo
Marvin, who provides us with an interesting contrast to Bob. The
movie sends the subtle message that Leo also is afraid of death, but
his coping mechanisms are different. To deal with his fear of death,
Leo seeks immortality. He wants to be as famous as Sigmund Freud.
Leo's way of denying the inevitable is through narcissism. Perhaps he
can escape being a mere mortal by becoming like a god. In the end,
Leo goes insane. He refuses to accept his limitations and doesn't seek
help from those around him.

Bob, on the other hand, accepts his limitations and seeks help
from outside of himself. He knows that life will be full of trials, he
knows that death is inevitable, and he knows that he's not strong
enough to deal with it on his own. That is why he's so persistent in
seeking help from Leo. He needs someone to be with him and to
help him. In the end, while Leo goes insane, Bob becomes healthy.[1]

The message of the movie is clear: those who replace the "when"
of trials with an "if" will drive themselves mad. If you think you can

avoid the fire and the water, then you're a fool. If you think you're above trials, then you'll go crazy. Embrace your mortality and your need for help, for then you will find it. The way to get through trials is to anticipate them.

This gives us a window into the nature of trials. Given that God anticipates your trials, they must have a purpose. At the heart of every trial is a beautiful opportunity, which we will see next.

TRUTH 2: GOD WILL BE WITH YOU IN YOUR TRIALS

There is nothing too scary for God. He is not a god who runs when he sees the water rising or seeks protection when the fire starts to burn. He doesn't limit himself to the sterile parts of our lives, when our affairs are in order and we're doing what we're supposed to be doing. "The one who is" is present with you through everything, to have and to hold, from this day forward, for better, for worse, for richer, for poorer, in sickness and in health. Nothing can stop him from being with you. Know that he will be with you like a strong and faithful husband.

Let me remind you of another popular movie, *The Notebook* (2004). It's about a 1940s gushing romance, but it's also the story of a modern-day elderly couple, as told by an old man named Duke to a woman named Allie, who's suffering from dementia. Before her old age and memory loss, she wrote down their story, the story of Noah (who is Duke) and Allie. She instructed Duke as follows: "Read this to me, and I'll come back to you." And that's exactly how the story unfolds. There is a moment when she breaks out of her dementia and she remembers her lover, but she soon relapses. Her memory and condition are so bad that someone begs Duke to leave her alone. They tell him to go home and take care of himself for a change. With passion and tenderness not easily forgotten, he proclaims, "She is my home!" He goes on, "That's my sweetheart in there. Wherever she is, that's where my home is." He stands by his words too, for the elderly couple soon dies peacefully in each other's arms.[2]

Nothing can stop the fidelity of true love, says the movie. Even when you're at your worst, able to give nothing in return, not even simple recognition, fidelity will stick with it. If this is how it happens in Hollywood, how much more will it happen in heaven? God makes good on his vow "I will be with you." He stays bedside of our misery, carefully reminding us of who we are, retelling our story together through his eyes.

Has the memory of your Beloved faded? Read the tattoos on your soul, and he'll come back to you. You can also read some of the gushing promises from Scripture: "In him you also are being built together into a dwelling place for God by the Spirit" (Eph. 2:22).

At first glance, this verse might not seem intimate—but take a closer look. This verse tells us that we are being made into a dwelling place for God. We are being made into *a home*. Don't overlook the tenderness of this expression. God is calling you his dwelling place, his home, just as Duke said of Allie. Has anyone ever called you his or her home before? This is not a tame expression; it's loaded with intentions and intimacy. It tastes of memory and love and experience. In our spiritual dementia, God says of us, "That's my sweetheart in there. Wherever she is, that's where my home is." *"I will be with you."*

God's people are being made into his dwelling place, his home. If no one else in your life desires you, know that God desires you. If no one else in your life wants to take you home, know that God wants to take you home. If no one else wants to live with you, in sickness and in health, for better or for worse, for richer or for poorer, know that God does. And death will never separate you from him. You won't die in each other's arms; you'll actually *live* in each other's arms—forever.

No trial can make you be homeless, for our dwelling place is with God.

Though the water will rise to the door, it will not envelop you.

TRUTH 3: TRIALS WILL NOT OVERWHELM YOU

Christina was proud of her mermaid tattoo. "I got this mermaid so that I will always have someone to rescue me when I'm drowning." With a clever smile, she showed me the brunette mermaid on her left bicep. I immediately thought of Isaiah 43:2, "When you pass through the waters, I will be with you; and through the rivers, they shall not overwhelm you." Christina's tattoo expresses the desire of our souls, which is to have a ready source of salvation to keep us from drowning when the water gets too high. I admit, having your own personal mermaid would be kind of cool, but then again, you'd only get to see it when life was rough!

You might wonder, *Since God says here that the flood or fire won't consume us, then does that mean that no harm will come to us?* No! Just think about the people to whom these words were originally spoken, the captive Israelites in Babylon. These people were already in the midst of a great trial. They were already experiencing the waves of the flood and the warmth of the fire. They had already been captured and dragged off by the enemy. The promise is not to keep them from the water and from the flames but to keep the water and flames from overwhelming them. God promises fire and he promises flood, but he also promises limits.

Your trial will get neither higher nor hotter than your capacity to endure it.

"But," you say, "what about those people whose hardships get too much for them to handle and they take their own lives?" I've known people who committed suicide because the flood seemed to be too great for them. Perhaps you have a loved one or a friend who did the same. They gave up on hope. It may seem like a cliché thing to say, but I am sorry for your loss. I wish that our loved ones would have trusted this promise from God. They may have been at the end of their resources, but they didn't know or couldn't grasp the significance that God wasn't at the end of his. I think of our Lord Jesus Christ. As the flood of beatings was raining down on his back, as the rusty spikes were being pounded into his hands, as he was being suspended by his own flesh on the cross, I wonder how many times he questioned whether God had run out of resources to save him. But God didn't run out then and he won't run out now.

Think of the word *hope* as an acronym, meaning "hold on, pain ends." Though the original shout of hope happened outside of the tomb when Jesus rose from the dead, echoes and whispers of hope reverberate throughout history, in every tomb since the first. Even the worst trials end in life. But not just in cases of death. The promise of hope is for every one of God's precious children who are in the midst of a flood. God will not give you more than you can handle. However, neither will God give you less than you can handle, as you rely on him. You will experience exile, but you won't experience it alone. You will experience hardship, but you won't experience it without the resources from God to help. The flood of his grace to help you is greater than the flood of the enemy to harm you. Long after the mermaid fails on your left arm, God will still be holding you up by his right. As it says just two chapters earlier in Isaiah, "Fear not, for I am with you; be not dismayed, for I am your God; I will strengthen you, I will help you, I will uphold you with my righteous right hand" (Isa. 41:10).

TRUTH 4: OUR FAITHLESSNESS DOES NOT STOP GOD'S FAITHFULNESS

If you could see my soul, I bet it would look black and blue, because I regularly beat myself up. Of course, it's a manner of speech, but do you know what I mean? I am hard on myself—I can't stand failure. My failures affect my relationship with God too. I often think something like this: *Since I failed in living up to God's standards, he won't want to have anything to do with me.* When I behave in a faithless way, I realize that God has every right to punish, reject, or leave me. That's what Scripture affirms too. In Isaiah 59:2, God said, "Your iniquities have made a separation between you and your God, and your sins have hidden his face from you so that he does not hear."

I know what my sins deserve. Actually, I know what they don't deserve: they don't deserve God. They have separated me from him, and he has every right to pay my wages their due.

Think about the story line behind our verses in Isaiah for a moment. God said, "I will be with you." But notice *when* he gave this promise. He didn't say it when his people were leaving Babylon and happily going home. He didn't say it as they were going out of slavery, having paid the penalty for their rebellion. Rather, God said this as his people were going *into* slavery! He made this promise as they were being hauled off to a foreign land as a consequence of their wicked lives.

God is not promising to be with us when we're finally out of slavery and have our lives back; God is promising to be with us when we're going into slavery, when our capture is fresh. When we're suffering from the consequences of our sin, God still loves us and is there for us. Imagine a judge who has sentenced a criminal to prison saying, "I am going with you!" You'd expect the judge to say, "I'll be there for you … once you get out." Instead, the judge does the unthinkable and joins the criminal as he goes to prison. In the same way, God doesn't allow us to face the consequences of our sins alone.

"But wait a minute," I can hear you say. "Isn't God the one who gave the consequences to begin with?" Yes. *That's right.*

This is an astonishing truth about our relationship with God. It's like the warm air of a radiator slipping quietly into the room on a cold day. It's a truth that Thomas Goodwin couldn't get over, dumbfounded by the fact that Jesus died in order to make us his friends when he could have made "new ones cheaper." Think about that for a moment. We learned how effortlessly God created the world in the beginning, so why didn't he just scrap this corrupt project—like a writer crinkling up a failed first draft—and start from scratch? Why lose sleep over it? Why lose blood, sweat, and tears over us? Why go to the cross for sinners like us? Why be faithful when we were faithless?

Our faithlessness doesn't stop his faithfulness. Meditate on our verse, savoring the order of its pronouns. "*I* will be with *you.*" God is the one who makes the first move. God is the one who puts forth the effort. God is the one who decides whether to leave us in our misery or to join us with his presence. "*I* will be with *you.*" That's how our relationship with God rolls. "I" before "you." God wants us to know that he calls us "friend" first, and our life with him is a consequence of this. In his grace, God has decided that he wants to be with us, and our infidelity can't stop his fidelity.

There's a ritual in the Old Testament known as the blood path that graphically illustrates this point. It's a ritual that two people participated in when they wanted to make a serious covenant with each other. In Genesis 15, God was preparing to enter into a covenant relationship with Abram, soon to be known as Abraham, promising him children, land, and blessing. A covenant was serious business; the roots of the word have to do with cutting. You could say that they were going to "cut a covenant" with each other. That's why God asked for some animals. He instructed Abram to cut the animals in half and spread the halves out evenly on the ground so that they formed a path. Picture a ladder lying down on the ground and you get the idea. The blood from the animals would then run together from each side, forming a warm, sticky, sweet-smelling path. Whoever was making the covenant was then supposed to walk down the path together, between the animal halves. Each person in the covenant was symbolically saying to the other, "May this happen to me if I break our covenant!" In other words, if one person didn't uphold his end of the promise, then he was saying, "Let me be ripped in half." As I said, a covenant is a serious deal.

After Abram cut the animals and spread them out to form a path, the sun went down and Abram fell into a deep sleep. More than that, we're told that a "dreadful and great darkness fell upon him" (Gen. 15:12). During the sleep, God made certain that Abram knew a little about his future. Abram and his people would one day be slaves in Egypt, but God would save them after four hundred years. Even more, God would judge their captors and allow Abram and his people to escape with the riches of Egypt. God wanted Abram to know that even when it seems as if God isn't upholding his end of the covenant, just wait. He will!

But then something amazing happened. Again, we're reminded that it was dark. God, who is represented by a "smoking fire pot and a flaming torch," passed between the pieces (Gen. 15:17). *God walked the blood path alone.* What was God saying to Abram? He was letting Abram know that he (God) alone would fulfill the promises of the covenant. If Abram and his future people broke their end of the covenant, God would pay the price. By walking down the blood path alone, God was committing to being ripped in half if Abram or his descendants were ever unfaithful.

Fast-forward to Babylon, where Abram's descendants, the people of Israel, sat in exile as a consequence to their unfaithfulness. Throughout their long and devastating history, they had broken covenant with God over and over again. They went after other gods, they sacrificed their children, they polluted the land with their idols, and they failed to uphold the law. From the very beginning, Abram's people broke their end of the deal. They deserved to be ripped in half, according to the vow made by their founder, Abram.

But only God walked down the sticky, sweet blood path that day. Now fast-forward to the cross. Before going to the cross, Jesus, the greatest Son of Abraham, lifted up a cup and said, "This cup is the *new covenant* in my blood" (1 Cor. 11:25). When did God bleed for our sins in order to uphold the covenant? On the cross of Jesus. Jesus was the Lamb whose body was torn in two, so that his blood could form a new path of grace that would lead sinners back to God. When we were fast asleep in our sin, surrounded by darkness, just as Abram was, Christ died for us and fulfilled the covenant. Our faithlessness did not stop his faithfulness. "*I* will be with *you*." God fulfilled every promise he ever made to us in Jesus.

Oftentimes, people get a tattoo identifying someone who is significant in their lives. I've met many couples who had matching tattoos. In a way, a tattoo is a self-inflicted wound that demonstrates commitment to another person. How much more do the wounds of Jesus demonstrate his commitment to us? His scars spell our names.

TRUTH 5: GOD WILL GIVE YOU ALL THAT YOU NEED

My friend Brandon is a captain in the army. Reflecting on his time in the Middle East, he once said to me, "Whenever I sent my soldiers out on a mission, I made sure that they had everything that they needed and that they were the kind of warriors who could be success-ful. I would not send them out unprepared. It was my job to make sure they had enough weapons and bullets and that they knew how to use them well." In the same way, when God sends his servants out on mission, he makes sure they have everything they need.

An incident in King David's life clearly illustrates this. David was fleeing from Saul and his army, but he had neither food nor weapon. God first provided bread for David (1 Sam. 21:1–6) and then a sword (vv. 8–9). These don't seem like much, but they were all that David needed. We're told that the sword God provided once belonged to Goliath of Gath. This was no strange coincidence, as it served as a powerful reminder to David. Just as God had been faithful to David in the past by helping him defeat the giant Goliath, so would God be faithful to David in his future trials. On a deeper level, God was also letting David know that there would be more fights to come.

In our journey with God, we need to have realistic expectations. God says to us, "Just because you're my child doesn't mean that life will be easy—it won't! It will be full of battles, for which you will need a sword." It's tempting to stop believing in God when we face hardship. *But trials might not be a sign that God has left you; trials might be a sign to start looking for what God has left you!* Has he left you bread? Has he left you a sword? Use them. God is training his servants to use what he has already provided. Revisit the resources that God has left with you. Perhaps the key to finding victory in your battles is closer than you think.

TRUTH 6: DON'T EXPECT FROM OTHERS WHAT ONLY GOD CAN GIVE

A friend of mine didn't like to wear his wedding ring because he worked with his hands for a living and didn't want to damage it. So he had an idea. He went into his local tattoo shop and asked if they could tattoo a ring on his finger. He thought it was a great idea, but the person working at the tattoo shop didn't agree. "We don't tattoo rings, because tattoos are forever." Bewildered, he thought, *As if my marriage isn't?*

The fact that a shop has a policy against giving wedding ring tattoos is definitely a commentary on our culture. Marriage should be forever. But I have to admit, the tattoo shop is right. Even the best marriages won't last forever. A seventy-year marriage will one day end, as the two are separated by death. While I disagree with the tattoo shop's policy, there is a kernel of truth in it.

We shouldn't expect from others the things that only God can give. This is especially true when it comes to fidelity. Other people will let us down, whether they mean to or not. Human promises are more like temporary tattoos in comparison to God's promises, which are like the real thing. Human loyalty can be fierce, but it's nothing compared with God's. The Israelites were hoping that Egypt would be there for them. God wanted his people to know that they would find no fidelity in Egypt. God said to their anxious hearts, "*I* will be with you."

In practice, we forget that people aren't God, so we end up placing massive expectations on them. Have you noticed that about yourself? I've noticed it in my life. I look to other people for validation, when all along I should be looking to God. I look to other people to comfort me, encourage me, and give me security, even though God has these for me too. Then, when other people inevitably fail me, I'm crushed. I have to remind myself that they're sinners, just as I am! Do you know what you can expect from sinners? Sin! Sometimes, our world needs to fall apart before we realize this truth, before we go to God for help. In this sense, exile can lead us to worship.

"Expect sin from sinners" is a good policy to abide by. It's especially helpful when you're involved in a local church. People often use negative experiences with others as excuses for not returning. "Did you see how she looked at me?" "Can you believe that nobody talked with me?" "I can't possibly go back after the hurt he caused us." While there are plenty of good reasons why you shouldn't go back to a particular church, your decision should be filtered through realistic expectations. If we think that unity comes to a church only when other humans stop sinning, we're seriously misguided. Unity doesn't come from others *not* letting you down; it comes from faithfulness. Other people will let us down, but will we be faithful?

The flip side to having realistic expectations when it comes to the church is also having a realistic solution. Isaiah discovered this solution when he approached the throne of God (Isa. 6:5). He confessed his own sin, "Woe is me! For I am lost!" but he didn't stop there. He also confessed the sins of his community. "I dwell in the midst of a people of unclean lips." While he had realistic expectations for his community, he didn't use them as an excuse to run away. He did the opposite. In genuine, heartfelt confession, he brought his community's sin before the throne of God to find forgiveness at the altar. We're summa cum laude when it comes to confessing our own sins, but when was the last time you wept over the sins of another? The deepest unity in a local church comes when the people huddle around the altar in genuine confession.

TRUTH 7: GOD HAS SOMETHING SPECIAL JUST FOR YOU

I noted that God's promise "I will be with you" is personal, but I don't think we fully realize how personal it is. God's great desire is to spend time with us in our trials. He has something just for you, which you can receive only in the furnace of affliction. It's no mistake that our verse says, "When you walk through fire you shall not be burned, and the flame shall not consume you." The mention of fire is supposed to provoke the memory of another incident in Israel's history when God's people were in the fire: Daniel 3 and Nebuchadnezzar's fiery furnace.

A handful of Israelites are the heroes of Daniel's book, which details their captivity in Babylon and their interactions with volatile King Nebuchadnezzar. Nebuchadnezzar made a colossal golden statue, which he commanded everyone in his kingdom to worship. Israelites named Shadrach, Meshach, and Abednego refused to comply, for they would worship no false gods. Nebuchadnezzar's policy stated that all who didn't worship the statue properly would be punished, so he had his guards throw the three rebels into a searing furnace. The furnace was so hot that his guards melted instantly when they threw Shadrach, Meshach, and Abednego through its doors. Then all of a sudden, Nebuchadnezzar witnessed a miracle: not only were the three unharmed by the flames, but also a fourth person was in the furnace with them. He exclaimed, "I see four men unbound, walking in the midst of the fire, and they are not hurt; and the appearance of the fourth is like a son of the gods" (Dan. 3:25). Note that they were walking in the fire. Also note that

God himself entered the furnace with the three, to keep them from being burned by the hungry fire. "When you *walk* through fire *you shall not be burned.*"

It is one thing to talk about the miracle itself, but it's another to talk about God's timing. Have you noticed how strange God's timing is? Do you wonder about the kinds of miracles God chooses to do? Why *this* miracle and not *that* one? If God knew he was going to perform a miracle to save the three Israelites, then why did he choose that particular one? God could have toppled the golden statue, plainly revealing that Nebuchadnezzar wasn't to be worshipped, vindicating the three in everyone's eyes. God could have caused Shadrach, Meshach, and Abednego to go unnoticed, slipping under the imperial radar. That would have been a miracle too. Or God could have caused the furnace to turn to ice before anyone was thrown into it. So why did he choose this rather dramatic miracle?

The answer has to do with God's peculiar, yet perfect, timing and his desire to be with us in our trials. God waited to strike with his miracle until the three were already in the fiery furnace—that fact alone should cause us to tremble with wonder. The miracle was to *preserve* them inside the furnace and be *present* with them in the fire. God wanted the fire to be a part of the equation. In this case, God didn't want to walk before them in order to keep them from trials, but he wanted to walk with them and protect them inside the trial. He wanted to experience their trial with them. God has a pattern of invading our distress rather than blocking it. When God does a miracle, it's often when our backs are against the ropes rather than when we're just entering the ring.

God often chooses to wait to rescue us because he has something for us to learn about him and experience with him. Have you ever wondered what the four talked about inside the furnace? Can you imagine being in such a scalding cauldron, having the sole attention of God? What did God say to them? What did they say to God? While we'll never know what they talked about, we do know one important fact: it was their special time with God, not ours. God reserved that moment just for them, and he has some special moments planned for you too.

The miracle God does in our trials isn't always the one we'd like him to do. God won't rewind your story so you can avoid going through a trial, nor will he always keep the trial from happening. More often, God will invade your trials in order to be inside the fire with you. These are special moments with God. Don't waste them. Talk with him, listen to him, and experience him in the flames, for this is a place of great spiritual clarity. God has something special just for you.

TRUTH 8: PRAYER FLOWS FROM FIDELITY

This brings us to the next truth about God's fidelity during our trials: the more we're aware of God's presence, the more we will pray. After all, we don't talk with those who aren't present with us in some way. Conversely, if we aren't praying, that reveals we don't believe that God is truly present. Lack of prayer assumes God's absence, just as active prayer assumes God's presence. Put poetically, *when we know that God is there, our voices will respond in prayer.* Fold your hands in prayer around God's promise of fidelity.

But what if I'm struggling with believing in God's existence? What if I live as if God isn't there? God's people ironically had the same problem. Though Israel acknowledged God with their lips, their hearts were far from him (Isa. 29:13). God said, "Their fear of me is a commandment taught by men." They didn't really believe in God; they just went along with the teaching of the status quo. When this happens to us, when our belief is shallow and unsubstantiated, one of the best things God can do is to lead us through the fire. When we're facing the fire, God becomes real to us; the ideas in our heads drop down into our hearts, shattering the doubt that stands as a barrier in between.

Have you ever noticed that about yourself? When trials come, we're suddenly interested in talking to God. We cry out to God for help, whether we previously acknowledged him or not. Some of my most unspiritual friends come to me for prayer when trials strike. Suddenly, God becomes real to them. Prayer is often the gateway to true faith. It's the doorway through which many people enter into a relationship with God. Reading the Bible is not their first step; prayer is. Meditating on the cross is not their first step; talking to God out of desperation is. Seeing a pastor is not their first step, begging a friend to intercede in prayer for them is. Prayer has a very important place in our faith journey.[3]

Some might object to this idea, thinking that it's not good to use God in this way, turning to him only when life gets tough. But I don't have a problem with it. After all, the essence of our sin and rebellion is pride, which is living for oneself and depending on one's own resources. To go to God out of desperation shows humility, the opposite of pride. Humility is admission that we don't have what it takes, that we're bankrupt and need a Redeemer. Pride keeps us in prayerlessness, relying on ourselves. When we pray, we enter into a world in which we have no control, where God is real and often wild. God delights when we turn to him in desperation. God hates when we refuse to acknowledge him; he especially despises when we use our religion as a cover-up. His cure for such lip service is often suffering.

"But if I pray, does that mean I'm weak?" Not according to Isaiah: "But they who wait for the LORD shall renew their strength; they shall mount up with wings like eagles; they shall run and not be weary; they shall walk and not faint" (Isa. 40:31).

The athlete who wants to be strong must work out; this is the only way to build physical muscle. The same is true with our souls. If we want strong souls, then we have to pray. As we talk with God, he will strengthen us. Those who don't pray will end up with flimsy souls. They will have neither the courage nor the strength to walk bravely through trials. They won't be able to stand up in times of suffering. Nobody will look to them for help, neither will they be able to give help to those in need.

TRUTH 9: TRIALS ARE NOT A DESTINATION BUT A PASSAGEWAY

When I was in college, a group of us went backpacking in Utah. Our leader was a recent veteran of Desert Storm and a very capable guide. However, due to some unusual conditions, one of the rivers that was usually quite low had risen high on the banks, masking the trail. The only way to the other side was to go through the river. Our leader gave us some important instructions before crossing. We had to hold our heavy backpacks over our heads to keep them out of the water, we were to help those who weren't strong enough, and so forth. I'll never forget the feeling of the rush of river water barreling against my chest, splashing in my mouth, as I held my pack high above my head. My feet stumbled for footing on the stony riverbed. At one point, one of my sandals started to slip off my foot, and I had to just drag it along. In addition to the heavy current, snakes were swimming in the water, coiling around our ankles, spiraling in and out of our steps. We were all quite relieved when the last person made it through the high waters!

Thankfully, we were not called to stay in the river. Our mission was to cross to the other side. We weren't called to remain in the thick surge, among the snarl of snakes. The river was a passageway, not our destination.

Notice the movement in our verse, as I highlight some of the key words for you:

> When you *pass through* the waters, I will be with you; and *through* the rivers, they shall not overwhelm you; when you *walk through* fire you shall not be burned, and the flame shall not consume you. (Isa. 43:2)

This is not a verse that finds us camping out in our trials, but one in which there is movement: *pass through* the waters; and *through* the rivers; and *walk through* the fire. Just as a group of backpackers isn't called to camp out in the rushing river, neither are God's children called to set up camp in suffering. Suffering is not our destination, but a passageway. Just as my goal was to get to the other side of the river, so is the Christian's goal to get to the other side of suffering. Don't fail to see the thrice-repeated word "through." God is saying to our hearts: you will get through this, you will get through this, you will get through this!

Suffering doesn't have the final say. Maybe you're holding everything above your head right now, feeling the snakes brush your skin—keep walking. *Don't quit.* God will get you through to the other side of this trial. It might feel as though your suffering will last forever, but it won't! Every trial has two banks—one where it begins and one where it ends.

This same truth comes out elsewhere in Scripture, as in Psalm 23, the well-known passage that says, "Even though I walk through the valley of the shadow of death, I will fear no evil, for you are with me" (v. 4). Notice the fidelity, "you are with me," and the movement, "I walk through the valley." As in Isaiah 43:2, we are not called to remain in the valley of the shadow of death, but to walk through it. "But," one might ask, "what about those who don't make it out of suffering? What about those who seem to suffer their whole lives and eventually die from disease or disability? Wouldn't you admit that they stay in suffering?" Psalm 23 is again helpful here, for it says, "Even though I walk through the valley of the *shadow* of death." When God walks by your side, death is turned into a mere shadow, having no substance to harm you ultimately. Charles Spurgeon wrote powerfully:

> For death in its substance has been removed, and
> only the shadow of it remains. Someone has said

that when there is a shadow there must be light
somewhere, and so there is. Death stands by the
side of the highway in which we have to travel,
and the light of heaven shining upon him throws
a shadow across our path; let us then rejoice that
there is a light beyond.

Nobody is afraid of a shadow, for a shadow
cannot stop a man's pathway even for a moment.
The shadow of a dog cannot bite; the shadow of
a sword cannot kill; the shadow of death cannot
destroy us. Let us not, therefore, be afraid.[4]

The ultimate river we must pass through is death, but we need
not be afraid even of that. We will also pass through death, trampling
it in our steps. We have confidence in this because of the one who
went before us, Jesus Christ. He was the first to pass through death,
opening the way for us to follow. My friend Tim illustrates this idea
with his kids by using a brown paper bag. He forms people out of
little pieces of paper and begins to put them in the bag. He tells
his kids that life was like this: Every single person went into death,
but nobody ever came out. Death collected everyone in its wicked
mouth. This all changed when Jesus died on the cross. Since Jesus
went into the bag with no sins of his own, death had nothing by
which to hold him. As a result, Jesus was able to come out of death.

However, at this point, Tim doesn't just pull Jesus out of the
bag's opening, as we might expect, for that's not what Jesus did. Jesus
didn't just back out of death, leaving all of us poor creatures inside.
Instead, Tim puts his fist inside the bag and punches a lethal hole

right through it. When he does this, all those who were in death escape out the back end, led by Jesus Christ, the one who opened the way, the Mighty Fist. Jesus broke through the grave and made it through to the other side of death. Those who hold on to Jesus don't remain in death; even death is a passageway to our true destination.

How much did this passageway cost us? It cost us nothing, but it cost Jesus everything.

TRUTH 10: FIDELITY IS COSTLY

Every time I walk down my street, I am reminded how costly fidelity is. My neighbors Paul and Joy have a sign in their front yard that reads:

Major Paul R. Syverson III
1971–2004
One of America's Best
His Life Reminds Us That Freedom Is Not Free

There's an incredible story behind that sign. Journalist Doug Stanton wrote a book called *Horse Soldiers* in which he described the true and riveting account of a small group of highly trained soldiers who invaded the mountains of Afghanistan to help the Northern Alliance fight against the Taliban.[5] Paul and Joy's son was one of these awesome "Horse Soldiers." Major Paul Syverson III was assigned to the army's elite Special Forces group, which was sent to Afghanistan as a direct response to the attacks on the United States on September 11, 2001. Virtually nobody knew about the secret mission of this group of soldiers, including their families. The conditions in which they had to operate were harsh, and the resources they used were crude. They rode around the desert on withered horses fighting against thousands of Taliban, drinking ditch water, and eating fried sheep. They used outdated and worn paper maps to call in bomb strikes from American jets flying above. One of their major achievements was to secure a Taliban city and regain a fort that had been taken by the terrorist group. The fight for the fort consisted of a few brave horse soldiers against six hundred armed Taliban.

Major Syverson was one of these heroes, and he was severely wounded by a bomb blast. After recovering, he served another mission in Iraq, where he died during a mortar attack on June 16, 2004. Ironically, among the ranks of the Taliban in the fort was an American from California. He was known to the Taliban as Abdul Hamid. He was part of the al-Qaeda army and Osama bin Laden's brigade. His name was John Walker Lindh. While Major Syverson was fighting for his country, Lindh was fighting against it. Syverson showed fidelity to the point of death; Lindh betrayed his own people.

Paul and Joy know intimately that fidelity to one's country is costly. In 2012, an anonymous donor gave them a beautiful bronze statue of a Horse Soldier, which is a replica of a larger statue in New York City. Though it sits on their mantel as a tribute to their son, it can't take his place at the table. Paul III was their only child. He was an accomplished musician, athlete, and community servant, well loved by all. Paul and Joy know what it's like to give up their greatest treasure in the name of fidelity. As their sign says, "Freedom is not free." Every time I walk by their home and see the American flag, I am reminded that they gave up their only son for my freedom.

Isaiah foresaw how costly fidelity would be for God. If he were going to redeem his people, he would have to pay. But what would it cost him? What would he choose to spend for us? Either he let creation go, falling completely from his merciful hand, or he let himself go. God knew that he would stand by his promise of "I will be with you." He knew that he was going to be faithful to his creation at the expense of himself. So he humbled himself, accommodating his divinity to our depravity, letting go of the former to save the latter. Isaiah described what he saw when God underwent what theologians call his "humiliation." "He had no form or majesty that we should look at him, and no beauty that we should desire him" (Isa. 53:2). In Isaiah's vision, he saw the unthinkable: God becoming flesh. All along, Isaiah realized that God was going to send a servant to save the Israelites from their suffering and sin. But he had no idea that our salvation would mean this.

When did the suffering of God begin? It didn't begin on the cross, but long before. It didn't begin when the authorities condemned him and beat him like an animal, but long before. It didn't begin when his friends and family rejected him, but long before. God's suffering began the moment he became a human being, assuming our mortality, to be with us. Just think about this: if I turned you into a worm to go fishing, your suffering would not start the moment you're cast in the water or the moment the fish bites down on you, but the moment you became a worm! In the same way, God's humiliation was the start of his suffering for humankind. Fidelity is costly. To be there for us, he had to forsake himself.

How did we respond to the incarnation of God's Son? Isaiah saw how we treated him, saying, "He was despised and rejected by men;

a man of sorrows, and acquainted with grief; and as one from whom men hide their faces he was despised, and we esteemed him not" (Isa. 53:3). God sent his own Son in human flesh to rescue us, and we despised him. Can you imagine what that must have been like? Have you ever been despised by those you came to help? Have you ever been rejected by the very ones you tried to accept?

Seeing our seething anger toward him and our rejection of him, he made up his mind. He still possessed the ability to call on heavenly forces for backup; he could still call down divine strikes on us rebels. But what did he do? Isaiah tells us: "Surely he has borne our griefs and carried our sorrows.... He was pierced for our transgressions; he was crushed for our iniquities; upon him was the chastisement that brought us peace, and with his wounds we are healed" (Isa. 53:4–5). God sent his Son to earth in order to absorb the wrath that was due to us. He became a worm so that death would have something to bite down on. God poured out his crushing wrath on his Son so we could go free. Fidelity is costly; our freedom was not free.

Isaiah wanted to be sure his readers understood this principle, so he added, "He was cut off out of the land of the living" (Isa. 53:8). The Savior was "cut off" so that sinners could be welcomed home. The Savior was pushed out so that we might be pulled in. When God said to us, "I will be with you," he meant no matter what. Even if it cost him his only Son, he would keep his promise. Jesus was cut off and crushed so that we could be redeemed and restored. Put another way, to save us from the rushing river, he was swept over; to shelter us from the consuming fire, he was burned. When God said, "I will be with you," he didn't just mean as another buddy, *but as our personal substitute.* He was swept over so that we could be swept in.

But it's not just that he paid the costly price for us; he also gave us his reward. He gave us the riches that he deserved for living a perfect life. He shared his "spoils of war" with us (see Isa. 53:12). He deposited his righteousness into our insolvent accounts (v. 11). He took away our sins and gave us his heavenly treasure. Why? Because the one who has written on our souls "I will be with you" loves us deeply.

TATTOO 3

I LOVE YOU

CHAPTER 6

THE OLD HEART AND ARROW

For I am the LORD *your God, the Holy One of Israel, your Savior.*
I give Egypt as your ransom, Cush and Seba in exchange for you.
Because you are precious in my eyes, and honored, and I love you,
I give men in return for you, peoples in exchange for your life.

Isaiah 43:3–4

THE HUMAN CONTRADICTION

Humans are a deep contradiction. On the one hand, we're completely narcissistic, doing everything in our ability to make this life about us; on the other hand, we know that if life were about us, we'd make a train wreck of it all. We long to be accepted, but we know that we are unacceptable. We are both beautiful and hideous, prone to flights of fancy and constantly gobbling up all the scraps we can find. There's a scene in *Good Morning, Vietnam*—one of the more powerful scenes in cinema—in which the horrors of war are casually shown on the screen while Louis Armstrong's "What a Wonderful World" plays in the background. That ironic scene captures the paradox of humanity: with hands around each other's necks in a stranglehold, eyes bulging, we sing to each other how wonderful life is. Even the idea of getting a tattoo reflects this contradiction; we want to do a certain kind of visceral violence to ourselves in order to express a deeper symbol—*significance through blood.*

Despite our earthiness, violence, and feelings of unacceptability, we're dying to know that it's not all a sham. It'd be easy to let our struggles speak the loudest, to let our finite humanity, squirming around in the blood of a million glitches, have the final say. It'd be easy to give up and resign, allowing evolution to run its violent course. But if we resign, we'll go crazy. Because we know that there's more to life than the fight of it all. We have dreams, hopes, imaginings, and longings. Our minds are seemingly unbounded, able to travel to heaven, the surreal, the past, the future, the perfect, and even the ridiculous with shocking ease. We can imagine possible worlds and impossible dreams. The only thing that seems to stop us is the fact that our freedom is constantly butting up against our fate. For all our crazy dreams, we have cruel limitations. As soon as we wake up in the morning, we realize how much we are bound by our bodies. They need to be cleaned, fed, toileted, mended, and rested. We can't just let ourselves go; we can't resign to living in a fantasy world, allowing our desires to soar like an eagle. The ultimate crisis of being human is the realization that though I feel eternal, I am actually marching closer to death each day.[1]

On the one hand, I am bound, mortal, unacceptable, limited, and falling short. On the other hand, I feel eternal, have dreams, have a conscience, have imaginative powers, and want to make this world a better place. The trouble is that these two poles exist in the same soul, namely mine. I know what's best, but I can't seem to do it. I want to be accepted, but I know that I'm unacceptable. I want to be free, but I keep doing what I don't want to do. I want to care for you, but I keep being careless in our relationship. I want to live up to my own expectations, but I have never done so a single day of my life. I dream of living forever, but every night's dream zaps another day from my life. I am a contradiction. Unless I can reconcile the two poles, I will go insane. Everything in me wants life, but everything around me spells death.

The only way to survive on this absurd journey is with love. Love reassures us and keeps us from going insane. Though I feel like a mere beast, love says, "I accept you anyway." Love helps us live and even thrive within our paradoxical skin. It is the deepest desire of our souls, because it helps us survive. Love is constantly negotiating between our ideal selves and our fallen selves. Love holds us together when we are on the verge of self-destruction. Love says to us, "I've got you."

This kind of love must not be generic, but personal. It must know who we are in order to accept us for who we are. It must make up for our defects and bridge the gap between the "who I am" and the "who I want to be." Love doesn't let me drift away into isolation and oblivion but intercepts me before it's too late. Pure love is personal. It is also *sacrificial*, *unconditional*, and *extravagant*.

MYSTERY

Our next soul tattoo reveals a great mystery to us. Here's what God says, "For I am the LORD your God, the Holy One of Israel, your Savior.... I love you" (Isa. 43:3–4).

The mystery is that God loves us. God wants to negotiate between our good selves and our fallen selves. He wants to fill in our gaps and hold us together. Now, when I call God's love a mystery, I do not mean that it's mysterious. Something that's mysterious can't be understood. God's love *can* be understood. In the Bible, a mystery is something that needs to be revealed. A good example of this is in Daniel 2, where King Nebuchadnezzar had a dream and demanded that someone explain it to him. But Nebuchadnezzar didn't just want someone to tell him what the dream meant; he wanted this person to tell him what his dream was in the first place. Everyone in the kingdom told him it was impossible to discern another man's dream. When Daniel heard about this problem, he sought the Lord for help. The Lord heard Daniel's prayer and acted on his behalf. "Then the mystery was revealed to Daniel in a vision of the night" (v. 19). A mystery is like a dream that needs to be revealed. Once it's revealed, you can know it.

God's love can be known. This is crucial for us to understand. We'll go searching for the soul-reconciling love that we long for but will always come up short so long as we look for it apart from God. We must realize that love like this can be found in the heart of God. It is his pleasure to reveal it to us. And even if it hasn't been revealed to you yet doesn't mean that it doesn't exist or can't be known.

FALSE FACE

This reminds me of a lesson I learned as a grocery clerk at our local market. It was my job to make sure that the aisles looked nice, which involved a technique called "false face." In order to make the shelves look full and pretty, the grocers were instructed to bring all the products to the front edge of the shelves, eliminating the appearance of emptiness. If a product were out of stock, instead of leaving a blank spot on the shelf, we were instructed to put another product in its place. For instance, if the relish were out of stock, then I'd fill the space with mustard, concealing the empty spot. That way, the shelf wouldn't look empty, which would be bad for business. Grocery stores don't want to give the impression that they're not well stocked, so each aisle puts on a false face when products are missing. A deceived customer is a happy customer.

If we're honest, we do the same thing with our souls. We put on a false face in order to conceal emptiness. We don't want to give the impression that we're not full, so we grab a bottle of mustard to fill the gap. Well, maybe not mustard, but we'll grab something—anything—just so long as it covers up the blankness. What do we grab? Material things, wealth, possessions. People, family, relationships, friends. Power, status, job, career, authority, accomplishments. Pleasure, gratification, adrenaline, substances. Religion, track records, morality, ethics. There is no limit to the things that we'll put on our shelves in order to conceal our emptiness. We're afraid of emptiness in part because we don't want others to know that we aren't full—that we don't have anything to offer, that we've run out, that we're not self-sufficient.

But we don't do this only for the sake of others; *we also do it for ourselves*. For the sake of my own sanity, I jam the shelves of my soul full of stuff—a positive ethic here and hardworking morale there. I'll load my soul with all its "pretties" so that I won't have to go to sleep at night thinking about the emptiness. I won't have to face the reality of my own condition, my own shortcomings, my own failures, my own littleness, and my own hollowness. We false face for others, but we mainly false face for ourselves.

MIRROR

One of the bravest things you can do is look in the mirror, and I mean really look. Look in such a way that you strip yourself bare of all your ridiculousness and all the ways you false face. You might think that doing so is narcissistic, and maybe it is, but only when you truly see yourself will you be able *not* to see yourself. I'm not just playing with words. We need to take an honest look in the mirror and realize what we are. We need to look past what we've managed to assemble and see the creature that is staring back at us. While the first glance at ourselves will make us appear larger than life, the longer we look, the smaller we become—the more realistic we become. One honest look in the mirror will level our shelves. That's why we pack our lives full of things: to numb our true condition and distract us from thinking about our fate.

MIDNIGHT MADNESS

I had just graduated from high school and was riding my bike at midnight down Taylor Road, an insignificant country road by my home. So many things were ringing in my ears that night. Polite applause and approval, yes, but also the fear of the unknown. I stopped my bike and stared up into the star-speckled sky. The sight stopped me dead in my tracks, holding me in its gaze. I was overwhelmed with the massiveness of everything compared with my finitude. I had just won some puny awards at graduation. I could still hear the nasally voice of one of my coworkers at the log home construction company telling me earlier that day, "Sammy, you're an all-American kid." But in the gaze of the stars, I felt as nothing. I was embarrassed in the presence of the galaxy, as if I had forgotten to put on clothes.

That night I had a frightening conversation with myself. I realized that if there were no God, I couldn't justify riding my bike another inch. I was paralyzed by the thought. The overwhelming sky, the coldness and darkness of it all were crushing. I felt as if I were on the conveyor belt of fate, which was slowly sending me to the black jaws of an impersonal universe. No awards could save me now. If there were no God, then I realized life was utterly absurd. No honest person could continue on with the thought of being so insignificant. I was tired of all the things I was hiding behind on the false shelves of my soul. I longed for the universe to be personal, for there to be a God who knew my name.

Hear the same longing in Percy Shelley's poem "Love's Philosophy":

> The fountains mingle with the river
>   And the rivers with the Ocean,
> The winds of Heaven mix for ever
>   With a sweet emotion;
> Nothing in the world is single;
>   All things by a law divine
> In one spirit meet and mingle.
>   Why not I with thine?—
>
> See the mountains kiss high Heaven
>   And the waves clasp one another;
> No sister-flower would be forgiven

> If it disdained its brother;
> And the sunlight clasps the earth
> And the moonbeams kiss the sea:
> What is all this sweet work worth
> If thou kiss not me?[2]

Shelley observed how nature interacts with itself. The wind mixes and mingles, the mountains soar to kiss heaven, the waves embrace each other, the sunlight blankets the ground. There are millions of indications that we live in a personal universe. But what's the point of life if I don't know that the Creator of life loves me? Life is not caring, but crushing, so long as the world is cold toward me. However, what if we aren't headed to fate's dark jaws but to the Creator's luminous lips? What if the universe really is personal and there really is a God for me to know? Only then would life be worth living.

TWO THINGS YOU MUST KNOW

John Calvin's massive theology book begins by saying that the most profound thing a person can do is grow in his knowledge of himself and his God.[3] The more we look in the mirror, the more we know about both. What does the mirror show us? The mirror shows us our sin, our disgusting patterns and habits. The mirror shows us our guilt, how we've compromised and what we've become. It shows us our smallness in the face of God's creation. There is really no good reason why the massiveness of the universe doesn't just swallow us up in an instant. Really. Just one random mishap of physics or chemistry, and we're history. Evaporated, flung into outer space, melted, frozen, crushed, starved, consumed, ripped in half. We are not safe, no matter what we tell ourselves. We don't want to admit this, but in the mirror we can't hide.

And the thought we try our best to fight away is that we're random. Why am I here? Am I arbitrary? Did my name need to exist? Could it just as easily not have existed? Does anyone really care? Will anyone really know or care about me a thousand years from now? Will anything I do be worth it? Am I a mistake?

Yes, the longer and harder we look, the more our egotism can't stand the pressure of being eclipsed by a massive universe. The harder we stare at ourselves and realize that we're only dust, the more we want to desist from making ourselves the center of life—the more we want to get out of our deadly self-spiral. Only then will we long for something or someone else to be at the center.

NAMES

Only when we take all of this in can we begin to understand the trembling tranquillity behind the third soul tattoo. It's trembling because the voice behind this statement belongs to God, the one who made the universe from nothing, who keeps track of every atom. Just in case we start to take God for granted, he reminds us by saying, "I am the LORD your God." He might as well have said, "I am the one who can put one hundred billion galaxies in my shirt pocket." If anything can eject us from the center of our self-orbit, it's this. When God comes at us, rolling out some of his many names, we understand that it's not the universe that defines us, but the Maker of the universe who does.

At the same time, this brings us tranquillity, as we learn that
the universe isn't impersonal, but personal. There's a face behind
every massive mountain and spectacular star. We're not on a deter-
ministic conveyor belt headed toward the dark jaws of fate; we are
in the hands of a personal being who wants to communicate with
us and who has a name. He is the one who has been with us this
whole time, who has kept us from being consumed. But there's
something else that is just as earth-shattering. It's the prospect that
the God who made it all has a list with our names on it.

Isaiah 43:3–4 is intensely personal. God isn't satisfied with
an abstract or distant relationship with us. The original Hebrew
places an emphasis on the pronoun "I" in verse 3. God says to
us, "For *I* am the LORD." The pronoun "I" necessitates a person,
not a force, not just raw power. Then God gave himself not just
one identification but four! He didn't merely say, "Hi, I am God,"
though that would have been more than enough. He went further and deeper with us. With every name he gave, he took off
a layer of mystery, revealing himself more and more. He called
himself Lord, God, Holy One, and Savior. He stripped himself of
unknowingness in order to embrace us with fuller intimacy. Then
he went so far as to link his identity with ours. He didn't just say
"Holy One" but "Holy One *of Israel*." He was using Israel's name
to reveal his. This is like a proud father at his son's football game,
when his son just scored the winning touchdown, saying, "I'm the
father of number fifty-two!" God linked his identity and even his
reputation with us, in effect saying, "I am not ashamed of these
my children." At our core, God wants us to know that we're in
this together.

THE CASTLE

Notice that God also called himself "your Savior." There's a powerful truth here that we must not miss. God's revelation of himself happens through salvation. The more God saves us, the more we know him. The more he saves us, the more personal his love becomes. The best way for you to know that the universe isn't impersonal is to look at salvation. Look at what God has done to rescue you from hopeless absurdity. When we're staring at the mirror, in the full realization that we don't stand a chance in this world on our own, God saves us and, in so doing, communicates to us that we're not alone.

Imagine that you live next door to a castle, one of those enormous fortresses from the Middle Ages. Though you live right next door, you've never seen the people who live in it. They are a mystery. For dozens of years, they never reveal themselves. Sure, you notice plenty of signs that they live there: the lawn is mowed, the garbage is put out, the exterior is maintained—you even see other people coming and going. But you never see the neighbors themselves.

One day, in the middle of the night, your house catches on fire. You wake up to a hopeless blaze. Your family is trapped. Just when you're about to give up, choking through the smoke comes an unfamiliar face. He is determined and strong, beckoning for you to rush into his arms. In an amazing feat, he rescues not only you but also your whole family, carrying you out of the flames. Only afterward do you discover that it was your neighbor. He revealed himself to you in the process of saving you. Were he not your savior, you would never have met him personally. Revelation was tied to salvation.

For many, God is a mysterious being who lives in a seemingly impenetrable castle. Though you see evidence of his existence, you never see him. There may be lots of good reasons to believe that he's a personal God, but as far as you know, he's not. That is, until you realize you're in desperate need and call on him. When he shows up, not only does he save you, but also you meet him.

Need leads to knowledge. God's people Israel knew God because he saved them, over and over again. He saved them from slavery in Egypt, and he was going to save them from Babylon. As salvation history has progressed, so has God's revelation of himself. Though we see hints of him throughout the Old Testament, not until we get to the rest of Scripture do we come face-to-face with the greatest revelation. The ultimate mystery is Jesus Christ and the Holy Spirit. God reveals himself to us as the Trinity: the Father, Son, and Holy Spirit. The Trinity is the economy of salvation worked out in history. When our heavenly neighbor, the definitive Good Samaritan, steps out of his castle in order to rescue us from our sin, we finally see him for what he really is. Listen to how one of the first disciples put it—you can almost hear the joyful discovery of this revelation in his words:

> That which was from the beginning, which we have heard, which we have seen with our eyes, which we looked upon and have touched with our hands, concerning the word of life—the life was made manifest, and we have seen it … and indeed our fellowship is with the Father and with his Son Jesus Christ. (1 John 1:1–3)

We meet God at last when we allow him to save us in the person of Jesus Christ. If you're swimming in the absurdity of life, repeating to yourself, "What is all this sweet work worth if thou kiss not me?" then the only way to find meaning is to embrace your poverty and dive into the mystery. When you stare into the mirror, stop faking it. Admit that you've been jamming your soul full of things that don't satisfy. Dare to let go of these idols and to stand alone in the presence of almighty God, the Holy One of Israel, your Savior. Then ask him to show you his personal love by saving you. We can't know him personally apart from our poverty and his remedy. There is no other way to escape the contradiction.

SLEEPING BEAUTY

French writer Charles Perrault (1628–1703) gave us the story of Sleeping Beauty. I know you've probably heard it dozens of times, but let's consider it again. Once upon a time there was a queen who had a beautiful daughter. When the girl was still a baby, a wicked witch put a curse on her, saying that on her sixteenth birthday she would prick her finger on a spindle and die. The queen was horrified. Then a good fairy came along and changed the spell so that the girl would not die but fall asleep. The only thing that could wake the girl was pure love.

Years went by and the little girl became a stunning young woman. Despite all of her mother's attempts to keep her away from spindles, on the girl's sixteenth birthday, she pricked her finger. At that moment, she fell into a deep sleep. When her mother heard the news, she came rushing in, doing everything she could think of to wake her up. But it was useless. There was nothing that she or the doctors and wizards could do. The queen asked the good fairy when her daughter would awake. The good fairy said, "She will awake in ten years or maybe one hundred; whenever she finds true love. A man with a pure heart must fall in love with her. Only that will bring her back to life." The queen angrily replied, "But who in his right mind would fall in love with a sleeping girl?"

More years passed, one hundred to be exact. As the story goes, a prince happened to be walking through the woods and noticed an abandoned castle. By now, due to the mother's grief and the passing of time, the castle had become overgrown. Nothing stirred within it. However, the prince couldn't help but let curiosity lead him to its doors. He managed to get inside and, after a little exploring, found the upstairs room where the princess was still fast asleep.

For a long time, the prince stood gazing at her lovely face. Overcome with emotion, he fell in love with her. Drawing close to her, he took the girl's hand in his and gently kissed it. Instantly, the princess opened her eyes, waking from her century-long sleep. Fluttering her eyes open and seeing the prince standing before her, she said quietly, "Oh, you have come at last! I have been waiting for you in my dream!"

The same is true with us. We have nothing to offer but our helplessness. We're fast asleep in our sins, and there is nothing about us that ought to cause our prince to fall in love with us. However, he has pure love, unlike anything we've ever known. The first mark of pure love is that it's *personal*, as we've seen in this chapter. Only this kind of love can wake us up and restore us to life.

It's a wonder that anyone would fall in love with us. Yet when God bends over our hollow, finite bodies and purses his lips to our hands, our hearts begin to stir. When he kisses our depravity with his divinity, our hearts begin to thump. The eyes of our hearts open, and we exclaim, "You're the one I've been dreaming of this whole time!"

The third tattoo written on your soul says, "I love you." These aren't words from another finite human who lives in a world that's out of his control. These unbelievable words come from the heart of God, who desires for you to know his personal love. It's as if he draws an arrow and pulls hard on his bow in order to send his love directly to your heart. He knows how much you need it, how much you've been dreaming about it, and how much sense it makes. Life doesn't make sense apart from God's personal love.

CHAPTER 7

CHOOSING JUST THE RIGHT ONE

For I am the LORD your God, the Holy One of Israel,
your Savior. I give Egypt as your ransom, Cush and
Seba in exchange for you. Because you are precious
in my eyes, and honored, and I love you, I give men
in return for you, peoples in exchange for your life.

Isaiah 43:3–4

CHOOSING

If you go into a tattoo shop, you will quickly learn that there are different types of tattoos. You can get a tattoo that falls into the "ancient" category. These are the oldest known designs. A modern US trend is to get a "tribal" tattoo, which imitates the bold lines of the ancient. There are also surreal tattoos that fall into the "biomechanical" category. These combine human and mechanical parts. The "photorealist" category aims at very realistic, portrait-quality images. Other trendy tattoos include those in the "Asian" category, which are mainly Japanese symbols. Similar to the Asian is the "design" category, which comprises tattoos of intricate designs and patterns. If these fail to satisfy, there is always the "traditional American" tattoo, which includes things such as skulls, knives, Betty Boop, anchors, "mom," and eagles. This category is still very popular.

Melissa had a tattoo of three stars on her hand. So did her husband, because they got them at the same time. Sadly, however, they divorced, and she was left with this permanent reminder of him on her skin. So she had the three stars turned into three birds. "The three birds stand for my three children; they are my three little birdies." While Melissa was able to morph her original tattoo into something else, there are many others who get tattoos only to regret them later.

As we learned earlier, God said to his people, "Behold, I have engraved you on the palms of my hands" (Isa. 49:16). It seems that God had to choose which tattoo to engrave too.[1] But how did he choose? What were his options? Understanding these questions will help us better grasp God's love for us. In the last chapter, we learned that God's love is personal. In this chapter, we'll learn a second thing about God's love: God's love is sacrificial. God's love chooses one and not another.

God didn't have to love us. Have you ever thought about that? He didn't have to create us, form us, redeem us, or call us. God could choose to love some and not others if he so desired. Knowing this makes the fact of his love all the more powerful. Consider this chilling verse: "For if God did not spare angels when they sinned, but cast them into hell and committed them to chains of gloomy darkness to be kept until the judgment" (2 Pet. 2:4).

According to this verse, God chose *not* to spare some of the angels who had sinned. He didn't give them his love but cast them into hell. If God is capable of doing this to the glorious angels, then who are we to presume that he will spare us? We'll never know how great God's love is until we realize that we are on the brink with the angels. Because of sin, nobody is safe. God doesn't *have* to choose us.

We need to live with a sense of "being on the brink." My goal is to be a spiritual optometrist, putting lenses over our eyes that can help us to see the true state of things. We need to look further into our spiritual crisis; we need to see the agony God went through when he chose us; we need to perceive the hopelessness of our bondage; we need to understand how costly it was to God. Think of a hardworking parent who labors to provide for the family. He or she toils during the day and during the night, doing whatever it takes. Often, the child has no idea how much the parent sacrifices to "make life happen." In fact, if children could really grasp the worries of a dad or the sacrifices of a mom, they would be stunned. How much more ought we be stunned when we realize how late God has stayed up for us? In fact, God never falls asleep on the job![2]

RANSOM

How does God love us? He gives things away for us, at great cost to himself. Isaiah 43:3 demonstrates this. God said to his people, "I give Egypt as your ransom, Cush and Seba in exchange for you." We first have to see that God owns Egypt, just as he owns every other nation. Every nation and people in the world are owned by God. God created Egypt, he sustained her, and he used her to do his will. On one level, Egypt was just as special to God as Israel was. Egypt was a great nation, full of sophistication, wealth, power, and resources. If Egypt were in your billfold, she'd have the face of Ben Franklin. She was a valuable part of God's world.

Israel, on the other hand, was a puny people, a bunch of alien slaves. In contrast to Egypt, nobody thought much of Israel (Deut. 7:7–8). The specific background to Isaiah 43:3 is the exodus of Israel from Egypt, during which time God's people served as slaves. No logical person would think that God would rescue little Israel at the great expense of Egypt. It would be like burning a hundred-dollar bill to save a five-dollar bill. But that's exactly what God did.

God spent his Egypt in order to save his Israel. He gave away Egypt for Israel's ransom. God also mentioned "Cush" and "Seba," which were areas at the extreme ends of Egypt, to illustrate that he had spent it all. He didn't leave any behind but drained Egypt to the dregs. God gave his Egypt for the people he had chosen.

What does it mean to ransom? We learned about the idea of ransom in chapter 3, when we discussed redemption. A ransom is the price paid to free someone from bondage. There are three crucial elements in our definition of ransom. First, there is *bondage*. Israel was in bondage, whether to Egypt or Babylon. We are in bondage to sin and death (so was Israel, for that matter). Second, there is our *inability*. People in bondage can't escape on their own. We can't gain our own freedom, lacking the resources, energy, and ability. Third, there is divine *costliness*. The ransom price must be drawn from God's account, coming at his expense rather than ours. These three elements are the foundation for a proper understanding of ransom. God gave his Egypt, all the way from Cush to Seba, in order to rescue us from bondage. Why? Because he loves us.

HOW HE LOVES US

Oftentimes, we equate "love" with "good." We believe that for God
to love us, then he has to do good things for us and give good things
to us. If we aren't getting what we think is good, then we feel God
isn't loving us. But he doesn't have to give us every possible good
thing in order to love us. That is a crucial truth. I believe a home,
health, and a stable income are good things, but God doesn't have
to give them to me for him to be good. "Love" doesn't always equal
my definition of "good." For instance, let's say that your foot is stuck
on the train tracks and a train is quickly approaching. Giving you a
friendly hug or a winning lottery ticket wouldn't be the most loving
action I could do at the moment. The best way to love you would be
to pull you off the tracks!

God's love always has in mind the oncoming train, whether
we perceive it or not. Though we don't always realize when we're
stuck on the tracks and though we can't see the approaching danger,
God does. His love reaches out accordingly, which is not always in
accordance with our assessment of "good." But when we put on our
spiritual glasses, we can see that the way God loves us is *very good.*
And the rapids we experience in life force us to cling to the rocks, lest
we plummet over the impending waterfall.

The best way for God to love us is to free us from our bondage. This doesn't necessarily mean that God gives Egypt in our stead.
Egypt is a metaphor for "something of great value." It's as if God
looked around heaven and said, "Who wants to be Egypt?" There was
only one Volunteer who had what it took to be Egypt. He stepped
forward and said, "Here am I. Send me."

There's another danger that we fall into when it comes to understanding God's love. The first had to do with equating "love" with "good." The second has to do with confusing quantity with quality. A good example of this confusion comes in our understanding of John 3:16. Here's how we often read this famous verse: "For God *so* loved the world, that he gave his only Son, that whoever believes in him should not perish but have eternal life." We think that the "so" stands for quantity, reading the verse like this: "God loved the world *so much* ..." We think the secret to God's love is found in the amount that he loved us. Then we repeat this to others, saying things like "Do you have any idea how much God loves you? God loves you *so* much!" We paint God's love in emotional terms, but freedom doesn't come from strong emotions. Just because we *really* love something doesn't mean that we actually change the circumstances. A mom could *really* want her son to be out of jail, but her intense emotions on the matter do little without bail money.

I'm not saying that God doesn't have a large quantity of love for us; he certainly does. But this understanding robs John 3:16 of its freeing power. While giving more love isn't a cure, giving a ransom is. The correct understanding of John 3:16 is to read "so" as an adverb of explanation. "God loved the world *in this way*, he gave his only Son ..." The "so" is meant to tell us how God loved the world. It doesn't refer to quantity, but quality. How did God love us? God loved us by giving his Son in our stead. Jesus is the one who stepped forward and said, "I will be Egypt." God's love for us is expressed in the giving of his Son for sinners.

Our culture is in love with the idea of a loving God. But God's love is more than just an emotional hurricane. We can get that kind of love from other sources. The kind of love we most need is the kind that only God gives. Maybe you've given up on God because you've been thinking about his love in quantitative terms. Start thinking differently today. God's love is a key that opens the door to salvation, to meaning, and to life.

EVIDENCE FROM HISTORY

Though today people long to believe in a God of love, this hasn't always been the case. In ancient times, it was believed that the gods would never love humans. Thinkers like Aristotle couldn't fathom the gods getting mixed up emotionally with mere creatures. It was almost unthinkable to believe that divinity could get jumbled up with depravity. So what changed? How is it that today we think God can love people, even more, that he *should* love people? Something had to have happened in history in order to cause this radical shift. Linguists find evidence for this shift in thought from the use of the word *agape*, which is one of the Greek words for *love*.

Before Jesus and the rise of Christianity, the word *agape* was rarely used; in fact, there are virtually no instances of *agape* in the ancient pagan literature.[3] However, after Jesus's life, death, and resurrection, the use of the word *agape* exploded in the writing of early Christians. If we're searching for the historical event where God's love broke through to humans, it would seem that Jesus's life is it. That's when the river broke through the dam. The word *agape* took on a new meaning, having to do with *the kind of love that reaches out sacrificially*, depending more on the strength of the lover and less on the qualities of the beloved. *Agape* found a way to answer the question "Can God love me?" by filtering itself through the sacrificial life of Jesus. Jesus is God's love for us.

THE FURNACE

Having discussed the quality of God's love, we can now appreciate the quantity of his love. The two come together during Jesus's prayer time on the Mount of Olives, just before he went to the cross.

> And he withdrew from them about a stone's throw, and knelt down and prayed, saying, "Father, if you are willing, remove this cup from me. Nevertheless, not my will, but yours, be done." And there appeared to him an angel from heaven, strengthening him. And being in an agony he prayed more earnestly; and his sweat became like great drops of blood falling down to the ground. (Luke 22:41–44)

"Is my sacrifice necessary?" Jesus pleaded with his heavenly Father. "Can't love be shown another way? Can't it be defined in any other way? Do I have to be given as the ransom price for sinners?" The moment was overwhelming, so much so that God had to send an angel to strengthen him. No human could bear the weight of this task. He was about to be thrown into the furnace of God's wrath.

Even if we remember that Jesus sacrificed himself for us, we fail to see that he *more than died*. Don't get me wrong; death is horrendous, but it's not as if it were a one-to-one operation: so that I don't have to die, Jesus died for me. It's not that shallow. When

Scripture speaks of Christ dying for sinners, the verb *die* carries a deeper definition. "In this is love, not that we have loved God but that he loved us and sent his Son to be the propitiation for our sins" (1 John 4:10). Jesus did not die as we die; he died as a *propitiation* for our sins. He became an offering in order to satisfy the wrath of God that is rightly due our sins. Jesus didn't just die for us; Jesus absorbed the eternal punishment for sins that we should have received. That's why he was in agony on the Mount of Olives, not because he was going to die—that would have been relatively easy—but because he was about to face the wrath of God for sinners. This is a completely different matter, more than the difference between the soft breath of a lover and the ripping strength of a tornado.

Jonathan Edwards put it vividly in his sermon "Christ's Agony." He envisioned Jesus praying to God in clear view of a blazing furnace of God's wrath. So Jesus agonized, feeling the heat of the approaching furnace. Which would he choose? Sinners or safety? Would he choose to save the world, or would he choose to save himself? Christ's agony was so great that, even with the angel's help, he began to sweat "great drops of blood." It's worth carefully reading an extended portion of Edwards's sermon:

> The strength of Christ's love more especially appears in this, that when he had such a full view of the dreadfulness of the cup that he was to drink, that so amazed him, he would notwithstanding even then take it up, and drink it. Then seems to have been the greatest and most peculiar trial of the strength of the love of Christ, when God set down the bitter portion

before him, and let him see what he had to drink, if
he persisted in his love to sinners; and brought him to
the mouth of the furnace that he might see its fierce-
ness, and have a full view of it, and have time then
to consider whether he would go in and suffer the
flames of this furnace for such unworthy creatures,
or not. This was as it were proposing it to Christ's last
consideration what he would do; as much as if it had
then been said to him, "Here is the cup that you are
to drink, unless you will give up your undertaking for
sinners, and even leave them to perish as they deserve.
Will you take this cup, and drink it for them, or not?
There is the furnace into which you are to be cast,
if they are to be saved; either they must perish, or
you must endure this for them. There you see how
terrible the heat of the furnace is; you see what pain
and anguish you must endure on the morrow, unless
you give up the cause of sinners. What will you do?
Is your love such that you will go on? Will you cast
yourself into this dreadful furnace of wrath?" Christ's
soul was overwhelmed with the thought; his feeble
human nature shrunk at the dismal sight. It put
him into this dreadful agony which you have heard
described; but his love to sinners held out.[4]

Edwards said that it's as if God brought Jesus in full view of the
furnace in order to show him what would happen if he persisted in
his love for sinners. Do you really want to suffer the wrath of God

for such unworthy creatures? Do you really want to suffer for people
who rape, murder, thieve, destroy, and terrorize? Are they worth
your precious life? Here's the cup of wrath that you will drink if you
continue in your quest to save these miserable mortals. Here's the
pain you will endure. *Is your love such that you will go on?* That was
the agonizing question Jesus sweat blood over. What kind of love did
he have? And would it be enough?

This leads us to think about the kind of love we seek. Do you
want merely emotional love? Are you sure? How about erotic love?
Are you positive? How about the kind of love that's full of stipula-
tions? What about the kind of love that friends share? Love that gives
you goose bumps? Will any of these forms of love help you withstand
the furnace of God's wrath?

At the edge of our seats, we wonder if Jesus will go through with
it. Will he drink the bitter cup? Will he march to the fated furnace? Is
Jesus's love strong enough for this wicked world? We hear Edwards's
victorious answer: *"But his love to sinners held out."* Don't you love
that? Jesus's love for you held out! It didn't compromise; it didn't
cave. Jesus said, "Yes! I will be Egypt!" In the end, the heat of Jesus's
love for you was greater than the heat of the furnace.

So Jesus went to the cross in order to die as the sacrifice for
sin, bearing the full weight of the wrath of God against sin. His
ransom on the cross paid for our freedom. *Only true love gives you
true freedom.* Jesus took your punishment, so there is no punishment
left for God's children. Unless we know the kind of love that takes
away punishment, we will never truly know any other kind of love.
Love will seem cheap, not deep. Our souls long for the kind of love
that is as "strong as death" (Song of Sol. 8:6).

THE STRENGTH OF HIS LOVE

In the film *Life of Pi*, Pi's family owns and operates a zoo. When he was a boy, Pi decided that he would like to feed their Bengal tiger. You see him with one of his little arms stretched through the iron bars of the gate, holding a chunk of raw meat. The Bengal tiger slowly approaches the bloody offering. Pi's body inches closer to the bars. The tiger creeps toward Pi. The scene is quiet, almost gentle, as the tiger eyes the meat. The boy's hand trembles with excitement, and his feet twitch nervously. Just as the tiger reaches his prize, Pi's father runs into the room, screaming. His aim is to scare the tiger away, and he is successful. The beast scampers out of the hallway.

Pi's dad is visibly and audibly angry. He scolds his son for being so careless and decides to teach him a lesson so he won't make the same mistake twice. His wife begs him not to do it, but Dad insists, ordering a small goat to be brought to the iron gate. He is resolute. "This is the only way he'll learn." The goat is tied to the gate; the tiger is released into the hallway. Just as before, the tiger methodically approaches the gate. The goat bleats in fear.

While I was watching the movie, I didn't see the point in the lesson. Why was the goat tied *outside* the bars? What was the point? Just to make sure the picture is clear in your mind, the goat was separated from the tiger by a heavy iron gate, whose bars were about four inches apart from each other.

Before you can think much further, the answer becomes clear. The tiger lunges toward the iron bars, the camera turns from the scene to hide its horror. The only thing you hear is rapid, dull thumping. When the camera returns to the cage, you see just the muscular back of the tiger, walking away from the gate. Only the rope remains attached to the bars, as the goat's body drapes limply from the tiger's incredible jaws. The great beast had pulled the goat through the iron bars, sucking it into its lair. Dad knew exactly what would have happened to his son.[5]

The Bengal tiger represents a powerful force. We are meant to be afraid of the tiger. As we've learned, it could be said that Jesus faced the tiger for us, being consumed so that we could go free. We're meant to be in awe of the tiger that defeated Jesus, ripping him from our hands. But there's an even greater force than the Bengal tiger. Imagine if the dad hadn't tied the goat to the gate. Imagine if the goat had walked willingly to the iron bars, using no rope to hold him there. He just stood bravely by, yes, trembling in fear, but holding out with great courage. Were he human, he would have sweat blood. Who would you be more afraid of in this hypothetical situation? The tiger or the goat?

The thoughtful person realizes that the greater power, in this imagined case, is found in the goat. The Bengal tiger is just doing what Bengal tigers do. The goat, on the other hand, is performing an unfathomable act of valor.

Jesus was the goat or, as he's also known, the Lamb. Jesus made it clear that no one needed to tie him to the gate; he went willingly.

> I lay down my life that I may take it up again. No one takes it from me, but I lay it down of my own accord. I have authority to lay it down, and I have authority to take it up again. (John 10:17–18)

The iron gate is the wooden cross, where Jesus went to face the wrath of God. Nobody forced his decision on the Mount of Olives where he sweat great drops of blood. He chose to go to the cross for us. His courage was much greater than the tiger's, just as the Lamb is stronger than death. Sacrifice is always stronger than death. The strongest kind of love has sacrifice at its core. Do you know this kind of love? It is tattooed on the soul of every person who has faith in Jesus Christ, "the Lamb of God, who takes away the sin of the world" (John 1:29). There is no stronger force in the cosmos than the love of Jesus for sinners. If you are afraid of the consequences of your sins, look to Jesus and you will soon be more "afraid" of the consequences of his love.

NEW LEASE ON LIFE

My favorite poet is George Herbert (1593–1633). I think you'll find the ideas in his poem "Redemption" to be quite telling:

> Having been tenant long to a rich Lord,
> Not thriving, I resolved to be bold,
> And make a suit unto him, to afford
> A new small-rented lease, and cancel th' old.
> In heaven at his manor I him sought:
> They told me there, that he was lately gone
> About some land, which he had dearly bought
> Long since on earth, to take possession.
> I straight return'd, and knowing his great birth,
> Sought him accordingly in great resorts;

In cities, theatres, gardens, parks, and courts:
At length I heard a ragged noise and mirth
Of thieves and murderers: there I him espied
Who straight, Your suit is granted, said, and died.[6]

Herbert raised an important question: How are you going to pay for your lease on life? One can't imagine living in a home without paying for it; someone *has* to pay the mortgage, the rent, or the lease. Those who don't pay will face the consequences. But what makes us think we can get away with living on earth without paying? What makes us think we can live at home in our bodies without paying the lease? The idea behind a lease is simple: I get the property and the landlord gets the payment. How are you going to pay for the "property" of you? Herbert's poem proposes two ways, the old way and the new way.

Actually, Herbert spoke of two kinds of leases, the old and the new. In the poem, the speaker is tired of the old lease. He is "not thriving" under its terms, and he wants to cancel it. We can relate to his discouragement. The old lease is the old way of trying to earn your stay through laborious works. You could summarize it with one word: *performance.* Those who perform well can stay; those who don't perform well will be shoved to the side. Can you relate? Life is constantly putting us under the magnifying glass of performance. "How do I stack up?" "Do I have what it takes?" Acceptance is based on performance. We labor under the terms of the old lease, striving to keep up with its demands, never really paying what we owe. So we fall further into debt, unable to escape the crushing weight of performance-based acceptance. Others tell us we're not good enough, not pretty enough, not successful enough, not talented enough. And in those rare moments when we aren't feeling the incredible pressures from others, we feel them from ourselves: we know we're guilty, having sinned against the Landlord over and over. All this is behind Herbert's choice of the words "not thriving." Because of this, he said, "I resolved to be bold." He would go to the rich Lord and ask for a new lease on life.

He called it a "new small-rented lease." At first we're not sure what he meant by this, but we can assume that it indicates that the terms will be different. So the speaker sets out to find the rich Lord. He goes to all the predictable places: "In heaven at his manor I him sought." The speaker knows that the Lord is of "great birth," so he looks for him in noble places: resorts, cities, theaters, gardens, parks, and courts. However, he can't find him in any of these places. In the meantime, he is told that long ago, the Lord left to go buy "dearly bought" land on earth. As the speaker is searching for the Lord in all the royal places on earth, some commotion finds his ear. He follows the "ragged noise" to a den of thieves and murderers. He stumbles upon a tavern brawl, only to find the rich Lord caught up in the middle of the mayhem.[7] As Shel Silverstein said in his poem made famous by Johnny Cash, he was rolling around in "the mud and the blood and the beer."[8] At the last moment, the Lord turns to the speaker, as if he were expecting him all along, and says, "Your suit is granted," and then he dies. Somehow, the rich Lord's fight to the death granted the speaker a new lease on life, canceling the old.

The key to getting a new lease on life is sacrifice. Long before God created the world, he determined to leave his heavenly manor in order to rescue us (2 Tim. 1:9). We don't have to go searching for him in inaccessible places, for he comes to us. He goes into the dirty places, where we are, the cracks and holes of society. One of the most compelling ideas in the Herbert poem is that before we are even aware of our debt, God has already left his heavenly manor to seek us out, to save us. While we were striving under the old lease, ignorant of any other option, Jesus left to redeem us. *Before we even know that we need him, he is dying for us in a fight.* What does his death accomplish? It pays the old lease, changing its terms, releasing us from its performance-based bondage. Now that the old lease is paid in full, we come under the terms of a new lease, that of grace.

Under the new lease of grace, we can stay on earth at the expense of our Lord. Even more, we can stay forever in our heavenly home with him. "For by grace you have been saved through faith. And this is not your own doing; it is the gift of God, not a result of works, so that no one may boast" (Eph. 2:8–9).

There is no boasting because of performance under the new lease; there is only celebration because of the gift of grace. The new terms of grace are tattooed on your soul. When life whispers to you, "You'll pay for that!" show your new lease signed with blood by the very Son of God.

CHAPTER 8

HOW IT LOOKS IN THE MIRROR

For I am the LORD your God, the Holy One of Israel,
your Savior. I give Egypt as your ransom, Cush and
Seba in exchange for you. Because you are precious in
my eyes, and honored, and I love you, I give men in
return for you, peoples in exchange for your life.

Isaiah 43:3–4

THE HOPELESS ROMANTIC

She had a fairly large tattoo, swirling with vivacious colors. It was of a beautiful face with endearing eyes yet a solemn smile. A banner that read "Hopeless Romantic" was draped over part of the face. The face on the tattoo matched the face of the young woman who wore it. Her name was Bobbi. It's certainly a bold move to get a tattoo of your own face, but Bobbi is not an arrogant person—quite the opposite actually. She is humble enough to admit that something is wrong. By painting herself as the hopeless romantic, she's not only taking ownership of the problem, but she is also confessing that she doesn't have what it takes to make it right. I wonder how many of us would be willing to be so indelibly candid.

"There is no hope for society," Bobbi told me. "People don't know what love is—at least not my generation." She paused, glanced at her boyfriend, and then added, "I'm twenty-four, and I guess I am a hopeless romantic." Some think that a hopeless romantic is a sentimental idealist, a person who is "in love with love." Bobbi is a realist; she has a different definition. In her understanding, a hopeless romantic is someone who craves true love but doesn't know where to find it. She knows it can't be found in society or culture. She wants love and believes in love, but she is convinced finding such love is a hopeless pursuit, especially among her generation. You might say that a hopeless romantic is someone who is not blind but still can't see.

Have you ever seen true love? Not the whitewashed stuff, but the real thing? Have you given up on finding true love? What if I were to tell you that true love is possible for you?

TRUE LOVE

There's a difference between human love and divine love. The kind of love that the God of the Bible gives depends on the perfection of the Lover rather than the imperfection of the beloved. Incomplete love, the kind of love we're used to, depends on the object of love. Think about the things that you love. Ask yourself if you love them as God loves you. If you say, "I love pizza," your love for pizza depends on the quality of the pizza. If pizza weren't somehow satisfying to you, then you wouldn't love it. Or how about "I love my dog"? Again, your love for the dog depends on the nature of the dog. Were the dog a fire-breathing monster, you wouldn't love him. Let's step it up one more notch; what if you say, "I love him" or "I love her"? Why do you love this person? Because of who that person is, right? The strength of human love depends on the character of the beloved, which in this case is the other person.

Return to the kind of love God has and you'll see a radical difference, which was unprecedented in antiquity. The pagan gods of old offered the kind of love that we're used to: conditional love. Their love depended on the character or nature of the object. They loved a human only when the person was a *good* human. The God of the Bible is radically different, for his love doesn't depend on the nature of the beloved, but on the perfection of himself.

God is perfect, and out of his perfection, he loves us, even though we are flawed. He has a strong character, and he uses his strong character to love those who are weak. This means that his love for us does not depend on our being lovable, or even worthy. We don't have to be "good" people for him to love us. We don't have to be perfect for him to love us. We could be lost in exile; we could be his vulgar enemies. We don't have to be beautiful for him to love us. We just have to be ourselves, for the kind of love God gives us depends more on him than us. This is called unconditional love.

You won't find this love anywhere else. It's radical and life transforming. You might be killing yourself in order to be pretty enough for someone else to love you. You might be trying to achieve enough success for someone else to love you. Perhaps you're convinced that being loved depends on you. That's certainly the kind of love that the world sells. But it's not true of the God who says, "You are precious in my eyes, and honored, and I love you."

In this chapter, we're going to examine these stunning sentiments from God. As we do, let me provide you with a quick paraphrase of his words so you can feel their effect in a fresh way. It's as if God said to his people in exile, *"You carry a lot of worth in my eyes, you are heavy-laden with beauty, and I love you."*

"YOU ARE"

Think about the "you" in Isaiah 43:4. Who was God addressing here? Superstars? Spiritual and moral wonders? At the beginning of Isaiah's book, we're told about the wretched condition of God's people. They're like children who have started a rebellion against their own dad (Isa. 1:2). Even worse, they're less faithful than farm animals. "The ox knows its owner, and the donkey its master's crib, but Israel does not know, my people do not understand" (v. 3). Isaiah sighed heavily as he said, "Ah, sinful nation, a people laden with iniquity, offspring of evildoers, children who deal corruptly! They have forsaken the LORD, they have despised the Holy One of Israel, they are utterly estranged" (v. 4). More than that, Isaiah said about them, "The whole head is sick.… From the sole of the foot even to the head, there is no soundness in it" (vv. 5–6). Picture a festering foot and a rotting face, a condition common to lepers—this is what Isaiah had in mind. God's people were far from superstars; they were terminal. Even at the end of Isaiah's book, the awful descriptions continue: "Your iniquities have made a separation between you and your God, and your sins have hidden his face from you so that he does not hear. For your hands are defiled with blood and your fingers with iniquity" (59:2–3). This was the sort of person God was addressing.

The text doesn't say, "You will be precious in my sight *after* you clean your life up a bit." It doesn't say, "You will be honored in my eyes *after* you perform some great deeds and gather a stellar list of achievements." God doesn't say, "I will love you *after* you become more faithful at following my commandments." Contrary to how our form of love works, God says, "You are already precious in my eyes, and honored, and I love you." God gives his future verdict on our lives in the present. We hear God's future judgment while we're still struggling and far from perfect.

Colin Smith, a pastor in the Chicago suburbs, said it's like knowing the results of an examination before you take it.[1] He spoke of the research degree that he completed in Great Britain. British degrees in advanced education don't have any course work; they depend entirely on research and the final examination interview. He was interviewed by two professors, one of whom was from the University of Oxford. You can imagine he was quite nervous with years of research hanging on his performance during a single interview. Could he defend his work? As he anxiously sat down with the two professors, the senior of the two immediately said to him, "We want you to know that we like your work and it meets the standard of the degree—so you can relax and enjoy this conversation." What an amazing gift!

This is an amazing gift that theologians call justification: God telling us in advance what he thinks of us. One day, we will all stand before God and have the opportunity to "defend" our work while on earth. There will be just one interview. But what if, before we even had the chance to start talking, God told us, "*You are precious in my eyes, and honored, and I love you*"? Hearing words like these would put our souls at rest, give us hope, and fill us with courage. Well, that's what God is telling us in Isaiah. So we can relax and "enjoy the conversation" with him during this life. "Justification is God's decision, made known in advance to all who are in Christ."[2] To be justified is to be made completely clean, just as if I'd never sinned. Only God lets his children know in advance how much he loves them. This means that even during our hardships and failures, God is holding on to us, and he will never let go.

Why must we agonize and wonder if we're precious in someone else's eyes when God has already spoken his ultimate verdict, the only one that really matters?

"PRECIOUS"

The Hebrew word for "precious" means to carry weight, to be scarce or esteemed. When something is precious, one places more value on it than on other things, making it "weighty." When "precious" appears in other Old Testament passages, it's surrounded by danger, notions of redemption, the human soul, and the eyes of the beholder (1 Sam. 26:21; 2 Kings 1:13–14; Ps. 49:8 KJV; 72:14). The precious soul must be saved before it's too late. When the word *precious* is called upon, it's usually because something is at stake.

What is at stake? According to Søren Kierkegaard, despair.[3] When humans are overwhelmed by their finitude and blemishes, they lose sense of their God-given greatness. We need to be reminded, lest we forget. After all, we were created in God's image; isn't that enough? Why do we weep over our appearance, struggle with acceptance, and burn with envy toward others? We were created in God's image! There's nothing nobler, more beautiful, or more stunning than that. Yet we treat our souls as if they were garbage. We desperately need to be reminded of the weight that our souls carry before it's too late.

I was waiting in line behind a man and his son at a café. The man was middle-aged and fairly rugged. His teenage son had Down syndrome, but his eyes were bright and he wore excitement on his face. Dad was getting him hot chocolate with whipped cream. As the two were waiting for the barista to hand them their drinks, the dad reached out his arm and placed his hand on the back of his son's hair. He gently folded his fingers into his son's hair and said, "Hey, beautiful." Both puzzled and innocent, the son answered simply, "What?" Staring deeply into his son's face, the dad said, "I love you."

This father saw the weight of his son's preciousness. In the world's eyes, this boy would never be a great athlete or a top student. He would never attain the world's standard of beauty. He'd probably live at home for longer than usual, depending on the care of his parents. He was most likely demanding and had surely required more of his parents as a baby. He probably had more than a few idiosyncrasies that tested his family's nerves. He was probably messy.[4]

But his dad loved him. His dad didn't label him as a burden, but as beautiful. His dad loved him just the way he was—I could see that plainly.

Our souls are sick from head to toe, yet our Father finds a way to love us anyway. Picture God raising his hand to your head and sifting your hair between his fingers. He looks into your eyes—knowing full well what you are—and says, "Hey, beautiful. I love you." That's enough to melt my heart in joy. There are no conditions to meet in order to earn God's love. He is in love with you just as you are. *"You carry a lot of worth in my eyes, you are heavy-laden with beauty, and I love you."*

"IN MY EYES"

If you get a tattoo, you will inevitably study it in the mirror. You'll assess how it looks in order to judge if it's "good" or "bad." As you decide this, you will begin to generate feelings for it, positive or negative. In the Bible, "eyes" represent perception, discernment, beauty, and emotion. The most important eyes in the Bible belong to God. Straight away, we're confronted with God's eyes. Genesis 1:4 says, "And God *saw* that the light was good." Over and over, after each thing that God created, he "saw" that it was good, whether land, vegetation, the sun, or the moon. Genesis 1 culminates after the creation of humans with "And God saw everything that he had made, and behold, it was very good" (v. 31).

When the serpent tempted Adam and Eve, he went for the eyes. He told Eve that God didn't want her eyes to "be opened" so that she might know good and evil (Gen. 3:5). Is it true? Did God not want humans to know about good and evil? Did he want us to stay in the dark? The careful reader will realize that the serpent, true to his ugly nature, was lying. *God had already shown Adam and Eve good and evil* when he told them that most trees were good, but one, the tree of the knowledge of good and evil, was bad (2:17). If they ate from this tree, they would "know" evil. In this sense, "know" doesn't mean mere knowledge, but rather experience. They already had the knowledge that they needed, but the serpent wanted them to gain the experience. He wanted them to rely on their own sight rather than God's. God said, "Don't eat it!" But Adam and Eve thought "it was a delight to the eyes" (3:6). In this thought, Adam and Eve entered into a cosmic staring contest between themselves and God. Whose vision would they trust? Would they trust God's eyes or their own? In the end, they trusted their own sight and ate of the forbidden tree, experiencing evil for the first time. And this first sight of evil has not ceased to flood the vision of humankind with darkness.

In Isaiah 43:4, we're brought back to our starting point: the eyes of God. Here we have the opportunity to reconnect with our Maker. Centuries of evil have blacked out the windows of our souls, but God's word is a lighthouse, whose beams can violate the darkness. We have another chance to trust God's vision when he says, "You are precious in my eyes, and honored, and I love you." Though we might have been away from God, his tender words welcome us back home. God is saying nothing new; he's only saying what he's said from the beginning. *Behold, you are very good.* We thought beauty was something that we had to earn, but it's really a pronouncement from God. The same God whose efficacious voice declared continents into existence has also pronounced your inherent preciousness. Just as sure as you can see a beautiful sunset, God looks at you and cries, "Glory!" Only the relentless lies of Satan keep us from believing this.

But how can this be? Doesn't God see our sins? In one sense, God has gone blind to our sins. He can't see our sins because he looks at our Savior, Jesus Christ. His eyes go to the cross and to the one who pleads our beauty before the throne.

"AND HONORED"

As with the word "precious," the idea behind the word "honor" has
to do with weight. Even more telling, the Hebrew word could also be
translated as "glory" or "beauty." To be honored is to be given glory.
The object of honor is weighed down with riches, heavy-laden with
worth and beauty. This seems unbelievable, until we remember the
cross and Jesus's magnificent redemption. Jesus bore on the tree our
dishonor and gave us his honor. He took on our ugly sin and gave us
his beautiful righteousness. But you don't get this beauty by pursuing
it; you get beauty by pursuing him.

Consider this story from Scripture. A sinful woman invaded the
home of a religious leader named Simon. Her goal was to find Jesus
so she could anoint his feet with perfume. Not only did she anoint
his feet with perfume, but she also wept on his feet and washed
them with her tears, drying them with her hair. When the grumpy
religious leader wondered about the sinful woman's actions, Jesus
told a parable. The story was about two men, one who was forgiven
a relatively small debt and the other who was forgiven a large debt.
Jesus then asked Simon this question, "Now which of them will love
[the moneylender] more?" The religious leader correctly responded,
"The one, I suppose, for whom he cancelled the larger debt" (Luke
7:42–43).

Jesus agreed with Simon and then went on to say how much
the woman was doing for him—anointing his feet and washing and
drying them—while Simon did nothing. The sinful woman was like
the person who had the large debt canceled, and the religious leader
was like the person who had the small debt canceled. The one who

had the larger debt canceled showed more love. And then, Jesus pronounced, "She has done a *beautiful* thing" (Mark 14:6).

Do you see? *When she stopped pursuing beauty, beauty started pursuing her.* She was truly beautiful because she lost herself in the love of her Savior. The more attention she gave to him, the more beautiful she became. Jesus honored her with his pronouncement of beauty.

Think about any modern female musician performing on a television music awards program. The culture may declare her beautiful, but is its assessment necessarily true? Honestly, do you think anyone will remember her performance five years from now? How about fifty years from now? I doubt it. Think of any provocative performance by today's supposed beauties. Will any of them be remembered a hundred years from now? How about two thousand years from now? Again, I seriously doubt it.

Now think about this sinful woman in Luke 7, and realize that the world is *still* enthralled by her "performance" of perfume and tears. What she did to Jesus two thousand years ago is as fresh as ever. Jesus even went so far as to say that she would be talked about until the end of time. "Truly, I say to you, wherever this gospel is proclaimed in the whole world, what she has done will also be told in memory of her" (Matt. 26:13). And it's true! There are billions and billions of Bibles around the world, each of which contains four accounts of her story![5] Not only is she remembered throughout the entire world (let's face it, she's gotten more press than any of today's celebrities) but also in perpetuity.

Do you know your debt? Even more, do you know that your entire debt has been canceled? *Do you know your forgiveness?* You are forgiven. Embrace that reality. If you trust in Jesus Christ to take away your debt, then he will! You are completely forgiven of all your past, present, and future sins. We'll never get beauty if we try to pursue it directly. True beauty comes when we lose ourselves in loving the only one who can wash away our sins. This is how he gives us honor.

"AND I LOVE YOU"

Have you ever thought about the purpose of love? Why does love exist? Notice I'm not just asking what love is but why there *is* love in the first place and *what* it is for. I guess there didn't have to be love; some other "thing" could have taken its place. Of course, we can't even begin to imagine what that other thing could have been. I do wonder, however, if any of the other great human and divine attributes could exist without love. Could hope exist without love? Or is hope somehow contingent on the existence of love? Could joy exist apart from love? How about peace? Love seems to be at the root of a lot of other attributes.

We could endlessly ponder what life would be like if love didn't exist, but I'd like to draw our attention to the purpose of love. Let's start by considering the importance of using things according to their purpose. Everything has a purpose; *purpose is an essential quality of a thing*. When we misuse something, we don't use it according to its purpose. If we use a rake to comb a child's hair, we're misusing the rake. That's not the purpose of a rake. If we use a golf club to brush our teeth, we're misusing the golf club. We're not using it according to its purpose. Often we can get away with misusing something, but in other instances, misusing something can be both harmful and destructive. This is especially true for something as important as love. The phrase "What is love?" was the most searched query on Google in 2012, showing us just how interested people are in this subject and revealing just how important a topic it is for us to explore.[6]

Relationship is the key to unlocking the purpose of love, for love assumes relationship. True love can't exist without another person. One may love oneself, but in the long run this is unnatural and unhealthy. Love needs another person as its object. Love wasn't meant to be another tool for taking care of oneself, but for taking care of others. I propose three main purposes of love: *expression*, *cohesion*, and *revitalization*. Each of these purposes assumes the presence of a relationship. "But can't someone just love himself?" Yes, but that's a weak version of the real thing, kind of like a person who plays catch with himself: while he can develop some skills, he definitely can't experience the full thing.

The first purpose of love is *expression*. In order to communicate or express our feelings toward others, we show love. Love is both an emotion and an action. While it can't be controlled as an emotion, it can be used as a tool in action. We can express our love to another by doing something for that person or saying particular words. Love allows the heart to vent its powerful emotions about the other.

The second purpose of love is *cohesion*. Love keeps people together when forces seek to rip them apart. In the Bible, love is painted with the strong brush of covenant. Love is more than a feeling; it's a commitment. Love says, "I promise to bind myself to you in a covenant relationship, and if I should break the terms of this contract, I will suffer the dire consequences." One of the purposes of love is to motivate us to cleave passionately to each other in unity.

The third broad purpose of love is *revitalization*. To revitalize is to put fresh wind in dead sails. Love seeks to make something that is weak or failing strong and successful. Love strives for the betterment of its object, whether a person or a thing. When you love another person, you serve, honor, protect, and help in whatever ways life demands. Love that focuses on the self is misused love; it may work for a while, but it never leads to joy. There are countless ways that love seeks to revitalize another; the opposite of love is not hatred, but selfishness.

When God says to us, "I love you," he has each of these purposes in mind. He is expressing his perfect emotion for us, he is showing his desire for cohesion with us, and he is seeking our revitalization. This is the transforming power of this soul tattoo. God's love is not only personal and sacrificial but also transformational. *God's love makes us better.* Before we met God, we were lost and condemned, but having found his love, we are precious and honored. If we don't allow God's love for us to transform us, we're misusing it.

Let me be abundantly clear: God loves you. This tattoo has the power to transform you completely, to bring to life whatever has died within you. Don't misuse God's love by thinking you have to earn it or by feeling you deserve it. Don't misuse his love by thinking that you're hopeless or that you've sinned too much. Don't misuse his love by neglecting to respond to it, by putting it off, or by quenching its fire when you feel it begin to warm your heart. Embrace God's love as fuel for transformation.

It's not that God's people are *just* forgiven or *just* loved, as if we're merely changed from slaves to neutral citizens. God's saving love does far more than erase our wrongs. God's love turns us into beautiful kings and queens, royalty in his kingdom. His love weighs us down with the beauty of Jesus, as his righteousness is credited to the accounts of our souls. Even more, because he loves us, he gives us the gift of the Holy Spirit, which is the presence of God in our lives, to encourage, strengthen, and lead us.

CHAPTER 9

IT WILL BE HARD TO HIDE

For I am the LORD your God, the Holy One of Israel, your Savior.
I give Egypt as your ransom, Cush and Seba in exchange for you.
Because you are precious in my eyes, and honored, and I love you,
I give men in return for you, peoples in exchange for your life.

Isaiah 43:3–4

YOU HAVE A SOUL

A popular trend is to get words or phrases tattooed on fitting areas of your body. For example, having "Free yourself" tattooed on your heels. You can imagine the thrill of being able to walk out of a rotten relationship with that tattoo. And who wouldn't notice "Stay strong" tattooed on your wrists, where it could be noticed when making a fist, the symbol of power? Or how about "Sometimes you've gotta fall before you fly" placed on the upper arm, right where wings would be—if humans had wings, that is?

I met a woman named Reanna who had "Love the life you live" on one shoulder and "Live the life you love" on the other. She told me, "I feel like I'm a really spiritual person. I got this quote from Bob Marley. It's about enjoying the life that you have. You might not have much, but you can enjoy what you have." By placing this tattoo across her shoulders, I imagine Reanna was making a statement about reaching out to embrace life.

In this chapter, we're focusing on the last sentence of Isaiah 43:4, which says, "I give men in return for you, peoples in exchange for your life." The word "life" is *nephesh*, which is the Hebrew word for "soul." *Nephesh* has a range of meanings, and certainly translating it as "life" here is fitting, but it has a deeper significance, which is its connection to the Divine. After all, why not just say "I give men in return for you, peoples in exchange for you" and leave out the word *nephesh*?

There is more to us than biology; there is *nephesh*. True, the word *nephesh* can refer to both human life and animal life. It means "living being." However, though it refers to both animals and humans, it's always tied to a single Maker, which is what makes it special. Rembrandt might paint a picture of an animal or a human; the significance is not necessarily the picture itself but the artist who painted the picture. That's where the painting gets its value. "It's a Rembrandt!" we declare. The significance of *nephesh* lies in the fact that God himself has created every living being.

Each of us has a *nephesh*, a soul, and it is hard to hide. We're constantly trying to satisfy it, and we're relentlessly expressing it, whether through tattoos or other means. Did you know this about your soul? And more importantly, do you know how to take care of your soul? Do you know what it needs? Do you know what makes it hurt? What makes it strong? I've found that though we study and know a lot about other things in life, we pay little attention to the study of our souls. The third soul tattoo is "I love you." We have learned that God's love is *personal, sacrificial,* and *transforming.* In this chapter, we will learn that God's love is also *extravagant.* These are words that our souls long to hear.

We can serve our souls in three ways: emotion, truth, and imagination.

EMOTION

"I give men in return for you, peoples in exchange for your life" contains a decent amount of emotion, doesn't it? You can imagine star-crossed lovers saying to each other, "I would give anything for you!" God says that he will give up human beings for us. That's intense! But before we get into the significance of such a statement, we need to talk about emotion. While we can't "force" our emotions, unless we're intentionally being deceptive, we *can* understand them and use them. Rather than letting our emotions get the upper hand on us, we can get the upper hand on our emotions. Sounds good, doesn't it?

We often fall into the trap of allowing our emotions to direct our future, when it's better to use our emotions to guide us in the present. Here's what I mean. Imagine an autumn day when the leaves are changing color. Would you ever look at the leaves and think, *Those color-changing leaves are causing the weather to turn cold?* Of course you wouldn't. The turning leaves do not cause the weather to change; rather, the changing weather causes the leaves to turn. Children might think that the leaves determine the weather, but they would eventually grow up and realize the foolishness of such a thought.

But when it comes to our emotions, sometimes we slip back into childish thinking. We spot emotions in our souls and begin to believe that they determine the weather. If we feel sorrow, we start to believe that our future is hopeless. If we're anxious, we think life is out to get us. If we're depressed, we think there's nothing to live for. If we're happy, we think things will turn out okay. We foolishly believe our emotions have the power to affect the climate of our lives. But let's remind ourselves of what we already know: Our emotions are like leaves. While they are a good indicator of the current climate *in* our lives, they do not determine the weather *of* our lives. The seasons of life are not controlled by how you feel. Just as a more powerful force determines the weather, so does a more powerful force determine the outcome of our lives.

Let me encourage you to trust what your emotions reveal to you, just as you trust the leaves to let you know what season it is; but don't put your trust *in* your emotions. Like leaves, our emotions will turn and come and go; they'll rustle with the passing wind, sometimes holding on, sometimes letting go. It's foolish to judge our lives by how we feel. If you're in a season of sadness right now, hold on, for the season will change. Today's sadness does not determine tomorrow's reality. God determines that. The seasons of our lives are in his caring hands. Ecclesiastes teaches us:

> For everything there is a season, and a time for
> every matter under heaven:
>
>   a time to be born, and a time to die;
>   a time to plant, and a time to pluck up what is
>   planted;
>   a time to kill, and a time to heal;

> a time to break down, and a time to build up;
> a time to weep and a time to laugh;
> a time to mourn, and a time to dance. (Eccl.
> 3:1–4)

Though our emotions are real and powerful, they don't have the final say on our lives. *Trust your emotions, but don't put your trust in your emotions.* Put your trust in the Lord Jesus Christ.

Our souls are like trees, and our emotions are like leaves. They can be beautiful or stark, arriving or departing, still or restless. While we shouldn't put our trust in our emotions, they can help us take care of our souls—but only when we learn to use them descriptively rather than prescriptively. To describe is to tell how something is. The condition of the leaves describes what the weather is like. To prescribe is to tell someone what to do. A doctor prescribes treatment, telling the patient what to do in order to get well. Use your emotions to describe the condition of your soul but not to prescribe the treatment. Think of a thermostat and a thermometer. A thermometer describes what the weather is like, while a thermostat prescribes what the temperature should be. A thermostat changes the temperature.

We are to use our emotions as a thermometer, not a thermostat. Go ahead and feel your emotions. Let them tell you what's going on in your soul. If the mercury in your thermometer rises to "happy," then experience the happiness. If the mercury sinks to "sad," then acknowledge the sadness. But don't allow emotions to set the temperature for your life. Just because you're sad doesn't mean that you need to set your life on "sad." That's not how it will always be. Just because you're angry doesn't mean that you must attack or take vengeance. Our emotions are neither omnipotent nor omniscient. They make good servants, but terrible masters.

TRUTH

Then how do we help our souls? We affect our souls by digesting the truth. If our emotions are the leaves and our souls are the trees, then the roots of our souls are grounded in our vision of reality—that is, our beliefs about what is real. They wrap around the stuff we put in our soil, seeking to find nutrients and sustenance. Why is that important? Well, the roots of our souls will absorb whatever we wrap them around. Bad food will result in poor spiritual health, while good food will lead to strong spiritual health. If you feed your roots bad food, the tree will weaken. A vigorous gust of wind has the potential to blow it over, the heart of the tree might rot, and the branches might not produce any fruit. Though our tendency is to focus on the leaves, we really should be focusing on the roots of our souls and learning how to feed them good food.

What do our roots need? They need truth. What is truth? Truth is whatever describes reality the best, whatever makes the most sense of the world. For instance, is there evil in this world? Some might argue no. But does a belief that evil exists line up best with what we know of reality? Yes. Therefore, we can assume it's true that there *is* evil in this world. Consider other important questions. Does God exist? Is there such a thing as right and wrong? Your vision of reality will help you discover answers to these questions.

I'm convinced that the Bible contains the best vision of reality. If we're looking for something that helps us make the best sense of our world—why things are the way they are—the Bible is our most faithful interpreter. It gives us the most compelling vision of reality. The Bible describes life as I've been describing it. Allow me to offer a quick recap. God created a good world, but the world became rebellious against its Maker, ushering in sin and death. God set apart some people to learn his ways, but they failed. So he sent his Son to succeed where humans miscarried. "Though God's people fail, God's Servant will prevail," as we've been learning. Jesus paid the penalty for our sinful rebellion on the cross, he defeated death, and he ascended into heaven, where he intercedes on behalf of his forgiven people. His people are being filled, guided, and emboldened by the Holy Spirit, who is reconciling the world to Christ. God will put the world to rights and then put an end to evil in a final judgment, though the final judgment has already taken place for those who are in Christ. Then he will dwell with his redeemed people for eternity, where they will enjoy the fruit and labors of the cross on a restored and renewed earth.

That's the Bible's vision of reality, which, I believe, makes the most sense of our careful observations of this world. There are plenty of other visions of reality in our world—atheism chief among them. But none of them accords as well with our observations of reality.

When we sink the roots of our souls into the truth found in Scripture, we begin to change for the good. Our souls revive, we gain wisdom, we find joy, and we become enlightened.

> The law of the LORD is perfect,
> *reviving* the soul;
> the testimony of the LORD is sure,
> making *wise* the simple;

the precepts of the LORD are right,

    rejoicing the heart;

the commandment of the LORD is pure,

    enlightening the eyes. (Ps. 19:7–8)

In these verses, law, testimony, precepts, and commandment all refer to the same thing: God's holy Word, in which we discover the truth. Do you see how sinking your roots into the truth of the Bible changes you? It revives your soul, makes you wise, gives you joy, and enlightens your heart.

The best way to handle your emotions and strengthen your soul is to remind yourself of the truth. When your emotions are being battered by the storms of life, sink your soul into Isaiah 43:1–7. Tell yourself over and over again the truth of what God says to us: "You are mine," "I will be with you," "I love you," and "I created you for my glory." Or go to Romans 8 and read the infinitely comforting words found in that chapter. You'll learn about the life you have in the Spirit, the prayers of Jesus on your behalf, our great hope, the help we have in weakness, the intercession of the cross, and the unquenchable love we have in Christ. You'll also learn that we are "more than conquerors through him who loved us" (v. 37). Sink your roots into the truths found in Scripture; trust the Bible, rather than your emotions or circumstances, to tell you about your life. You will discover that you are beautiful, that you are royalty, that you are completely forgiven, that you have purpose, that you have hope, and that you are loved unconditionally. The weather will change, but God's Word will remain firm. "The grass withers, the flower fades, but the word of our God will stand forever" (Isa. 40:8).

IMAGINATION

There's another way to affect your soul, which is not an alternative to the truth, but a way of laying hold of it. Maybe we're convinced that our souls need the truth, but our roots have no desire to let go of their idols in order to embrace God's truth. What do we do then? How can we convince our souls to believe the promises of Scripture and live according to their vision of reality? Tim Keller wrote a helpful article that teaches us the vital role of imagination. In order to "convince" your soul to grab hold of truth, you need to use your imagination. Imagination is more fundamental to the human soul than truth; it's the vehicle that transports truth to the human understanding. Imagination is like a conveyor belt that carries possibilities to the mind for the human reason to consider. It's like a lawyer who argues for one vision of reality over another, convincing us that one is better than the other. Puritan Richard Sibbes called imagination the "power of the soul." And Keller expanded on the Puritan understanding of imagination:

> Imagine two thoughts sitting on the intellect: "This sin will feel good if I do it" and "This sin will displease God if I do it." Both are facts in the mind. You believe both to be true. But which one will control your heart? That is, which one will capture your thinking, your emotions, and your will?
>
> The Puritan answer: the one that possesses the imagination will control the mind, will, and emotions (all three will be captured at once).[1]

I've found this to be extremely profound and practically helpful. Our imaginations help us choose the truth that will please
God. How do we choose between two thoughts that appear equally
true? We choose the one that is more real to us. But how does
one "truth" or thought become more real than the other? Through
imagination! To imagine means to make one thing more real, more
vivid, than something else. Your imagination will argue the case in
your head, eventually making one option more compelling than
the other. And that's where you'll sink the roots of your soul.

Look again at Keller's example of two competing truths we
often wrestle with in our imaginations: "This sin will feel good if I
do it" versus "This sin will displease God if I do it." Both are true.
We do "feel good" when we make some sinful choices. But it's also
true that God abhors sin. So which will you grab hold of? Let's say
that your imagination makes the sin more real, more vivid, and
more desirable. When the promise of "feeling good" becomes the
greater truth, that's what you'll choose. On the other hand, your
imagination can also make God more real, more vivid, and more
desirable to you so that you want nothing more than to please your
heavenly Father. When that happens, you choose obedience rather
than sin.

When it comes to growing a healthy soul, *we must water the
ground with imagination.* To summarize this metaphor: your emotions are the leaves, your soul is the tree, the roots of your soul are
sunk into the soil of the truth, and imagination is the water you pour
into the soil. We must use our imaginations to embrace the truths
we find in Scripture, making them become weightier and richer in
our hearts than anything else. The more vivid they become to us,

the more we will choose them, and then the stronger our souls will become.

Too often we have a failure of imagination. We'll read a book, hear something gripping at church, or run across a Bible verse that tugs at our hearts, but we'll fail to ask the simple question, "What if?" What if this promise really is true? What if this vision of reality is true? What if I really am loved like this? We fail to water the good news of Jesus Christ, leaving our soil parched and our roots shriveled and our souls dead.

EXTRAVAGANCE

I say all of this to prepare us for the conclusion of Isaiah 43:4, which says, "I give men in return for you, peoples in exchange for your life." What if this were true? Can you imagine it to be true? This part of the verse opens by saying, "I give men in return for you," but then the language ramps up and God confesses that he actually gave many "peoples in exchange for your life." God wants us to know the extravagance of his gift for us. The phrases "in return for" and "in exchange for" mean the same thing. The Hebrew word *tachath* carries the meaning of "below" or "beneath." Picture one person shoving another below the water, submerging his head beneath the surface. It's as if God says that he shoved one person beneath the water so that the other could rise to life. That's what it means to give one in exchange for another.

God gave away Egypt for his people, as we learned in the last chapter. He ransomed his people from the clutches of Pharaoh, destroying all the firstborn of Egypt in the process. God was quite right when he said he had given away "people." As we know from the fuller revelation of Scripture, God gave away the Cosmic Firstborn for us, the object of his eternal affection, his own Son. The most extravagant gift that the world has ever known is Jesus Christ. While most of us want to "live life to the full," the mission of God in Christ was to "live life to be emptied." In order to come and rescue us, God had to empty himself of his glory and die in submission to our curse. Jesus plunged beneath the water so that we could be rescued from drowning.

THE PERFORMANCE TO DYING MEN

Who can forget the scene near the end of Elie Wiesel's *Night*, the true account of his experiences in Nazi death camps? The Nazis were forcing their Jewish prisoners to march many miles in the biting winter to Gleiwitz. When the prisoners finally arrived, many having died along the way, they were shoved into a shed, bodies piled on top of one another. Inside the stinking shed, Elie heard a familiar voice belonging to another boy named Juliek, who was his friend from a former camp. To Elie's astonishment, Juliek had managed to bring his violin, though bodies were on the verge of crushing one another. As the hours and oxygen slipped away, and as the prisoners fought against sleep for fear that death would take them, the sound of the violin unexpectedly ascended from the mass of bodies. "The sound of a violin, in this dark shed, where the dead were heaped on the living. What madman could be playing the violin here, at the brink of his own grave?" It was Juliek, who defiantly had begun to play a fragment from Beethoven's concerto. Listen to Wiesel's gripping description:

> It was pitch dark. I could hear only the violin, and it was as though Juliek's soul were the bow. He was playing his life. The whole of his life was gliding on the strings—his lost hopes, his charred past, his extinguished future. He played as he would never play again.... I shall never forget Juliek. How could I forget that concert, given to an audience of dying and dead men![2]

When Elie woke the next morning, Juliek was slumped over, dead; his violin was smashed on the ground next to him.

This gives us a picture of the extravagant love of Jesus Christ, who played his soul on the cross for us. Can you imagine the music? Jesus's concert was to "dying and dead men," because he was surrounded by an audience of two crucified criminals. Nobody cheered for him; there were only shouts of disgust and rage. But Jesus played on. The criminals began to argue about the performance. One of them mocked him, but the other believed in him. "Do you not fear God, since you are under the same sentence of condemnation?" he said to the one who mocked (Luke 23:40). It was an atrocity of judgment to see that Jesus was given the same sentence as these other two. Not only had Jesus done nothing wrong, but also he was a powerful healer, known for his spiritual devotion and godliness. Then the criminal confessed, "And we indeed justly, for we are receiving the due reward of our deeds; but this man has done nothing wrong"

(v. 41). He admitted that they were getting what they deserved; he also showed his belief that Jesus was innocent. During this exchange, Jesus remained silent, pulling each painful note of forgiveness as his soul slid against the rugged wood. He managed to stay in complete harmony with his Father's will.

The criminal who believed then spoke to Jesus, "Jesus, remember me when you come into your kingdom" (v. 42). I suspect the criminal didn't expect a response. After all, who was he but a run-of-the-mill thief that the Son of God should give him the time of day? At least he recognized that Jesus was a king. After all the beatings and blood loss, and the effort it took to keep breathing as asphyxiation drew near, Jesus was probably struggling to retain consciousness. It was enough effort just to catch a single breath; he surely didn't owe a response to this criminal. No king would.

But then, unexpectedly, came the raspy voice of Jesus offering a response between agonizing breaths: "Truly, I say to you, today you will be with me in Paradise" (v. 43). That was the sweetest song the criminal had ever heard. Can you imagine? Today? Today was the worst day of the criminal's life—it was also the last day! And on the very worst day of his life, he would enter into the very best day of his life. The criminal knew he didn't have what it would take to enter into paradise; he needed righteousness for that. If Adam and Eve were kicked out of their paradise for just one act of sin, then this criminal had no right to enter paradise after a whole lifetime of sin. But Jesus was giving him exactly what he needed. *Jesus was his gift of righteousness.*

Just as Jesus was giving his performance to the criminal, the criminal was entering into Jesus's performance. The two were becoming one. Jesus was taking on the sins of the criminal; the criminal was taking on the perfection of Jesus. They suffered together, they would die together, they would rise together, and they would enter paradise together. Jesus acknowledged on the cross simply what the apostle Paul would pick up on later. Jesus said to the criminal, "You will be with me."

The phrase "with me" is loaded with significance throughout the New Testament. Paul helps us understand this "with me" or "with Christ" formula as meaning that whatever happens to Jesus happens to Christians. It's similar to the scene in the classic movie *E. T.* where Elliott and E.T. become "one" with each other. Whatever happens to one happens simultaneously to the other. When E.T. is drunk, Elliott is drunk (a great kids movie!); when E.T. is sick, Elliott is sick; when E.T. is dying, Elliott is dying; and when E.T. gets well, Elliott gets well.[3] If Jesus dies on the cross for sins, then Christians die on the cross for sins. If Jesus rises from the grave, then Christians rise from the grave. If Jesus ascends to glory in heaven, then Christians ascend to glory in heaven. Christ's life becomes ours, just as our sin and death became his. The apostle Paul put it this way:

> If then you have been raised with Christ … For you
> have died, and your life is hidden with Christ in
> God. When Christ who is your life appears, then you
> also will appear with him in glory. (Col. 3:1, 3–4)

Our lives are hidden with Christ, and when he appears in glory—or paradise—so will we. Can you think of a more extravagant performance of love? His performance on the cross brings us into the paradise we've been searching for our whole lives. It's the place in which our souls were truly meant to dwell and thrive.

What "madman" could play the song of salvation at a time like this, when his soul was being battered by divine wrath against human sin? His name is Jesus, the gift and giver of extravagant love. *"I give men in return for you."* If you know this love, then it will be hard to hide.

This brings us to our final soul tattoo, "I created you for my glory."

TATTOO 4

I CREATED YOU
FOR MY GLORY

CHAPTER 10

YOU WILL NEVER BE THE SAME

Fear not, for I am with you; I will bring your
offspring from the east, and from the west I will
gather you. I will say to the north, Give up, and
to the south, Do not withhold; bring my sons
from afar and my daughters from the end of the
earth, everyone who is called by my name, whom I
created for my glory, whom I formed and made.

Isaiah 43:5–7

YOU CAN'T GO BACK

Getting a tattoo isn't like trying out a new haircut, which you can change once your hair grows back. Nor is it like wearing the latest fashion, which you can don every time a new trend comes along. It's more than switching from glasses to contact lenses or going from pale to tan. Tattoos are for those who are willing to change themselves permanently.

I met a guy named David who had a tattoo on each of his forearms. On his right forearm, tattooed in an unusual font, was the word "Purity." On his left forearm was a tattoo of a family crest, which represented a seal of marriage with his wife. Every day of his life, these tattoos reminded David of his vows to his wife for purity and commitment. He didn't want to go back to his old days of being single and uncommitted; he chose to go in a different direction—for good.

If you and I want to have a relationship with God, then our lives will be changed, not temporarily, but permanently. If we truly realize all the promises that God has tattooed on our souls, then there's no going back. The person who boasts the tattoo "You are mine" is permanently changed. The one who wears the tattoo "I will be with you" will never be the same again. The soul who carries with it "I love you" realizes that life is forever different. They have these stains that are much deeper than scars.

We arrive now at our final soul tattoo, "I created you for my glory." This, too, will change you. In fact, we need to see its transformative power if we're going to understand what it means. Christianity is all about renovation, about taking us from point A to point B, and eventually all the way to Z! While it has been wonderful to learn about the first three tattoos, if we stopped here, the whole thing would collapse. Some might be tempted to skip this last tattoo, since it might seem too vague or religious. But doing so would be toxic to our faith. Imagine being healed from a deadly disease. After massive efforts to help you, the physician tells you to leave the environment in which you've been living. But you like where you live. You don't want to move. Guess what? It's only a matter of time before you're back in the hospital suffering from the very same disease. This is true in our spiritual lives too. Even though you came so far, your failure to obey the command to leave your old life could kill you. "I love you" means nothing without "I created you for my glory."

WHAT IS GOD'S GLORY?

God's glory is his holiness put on display. This will seem abstract only until you encounter it. Then it will become the most breathtaking reality in your life. You'll never be the same again, and everything will be put back into correct perspective. God's glory must be the vantage point from which we look at all of life. If we don't encounter God's glory, then everything else will be skewed, because everything else will seem more important than God.

Many are familiar with outdoor music festivals. The oldest one in the United States is just down the road from me. It's called Ravinia. Since 1904, Ravinia has hosted world-class music events day after day through the summer months. Imagine if you lived next to Ravinia but for some reason never knew it. Almost daily, you would hear traces of the music but never realize where it was coming from. If you never ventured away from your home, you might just assume that the wonderful sounds were a part of nature, maybe something enchanting about how the wind blew across the gutters. What if you never set out to discover where all the music had been coming from your whole life? Well, you never would have had the pleasure of enjoying a wonderful concert, never would have picnicked on the lawn with your friends or breathed in the animated air of festival life. Instead, you would only have heard the faint echoes of instruments and singing, joy and laughter, never tasting them for yourself.

God's glory is all around us, as faint music, whispering through the woods. But do we know what it is? Do we know where it's coming from? What if we could discover it? This is what happened to Isaiah. He found himself center stage in the great concert of God's glory. Here's how Isaiah described it:

> In the year that King Uzziah died I saw the Lord sitting upon a throne, high and lifted up; and the train of his robe filled the temple. Above him stood the seraphim. Each had six wings: with two he covered his face, and with two he covered his feet, and with two he flew. And one called to another and said:
>
> "Holy, holy, holy is the LORD of hosts;
> the whole earth is full of his glory!"
>
> And the foundations of the thresholds shook at the voice of him who called, and the house was filled with smoke. (Isa. 6:1–4)

Like Ravinia, this concert was beautiful, but unlike Ravinia, it wasn't safe. This concert of glory was tremendous and terrifying. That's because it's the concert of God's holiness. Before we think, *I could never afford to get admission into a concert like this! My life would have to be neat and tidy before receiving this kind of invitation!* consider the setting: The verse just before this informs us that the whole land was full of growling, darkness, and distress (Isa.

5:30). Even more, we're told that Uzziah, the one who had been king for fifty-two years, had died. When we get a little further into the story, we'll see that Isaiah himself fell over as if dead. All this to say, suffering and death are present in abundance, so there is nothing particularly "holy" about the circumstances. It seems that *anyone*, so long as you know something of suffering or death, can get into this concert. Once admitted, you witness a sight that is best described as *numinous*.

Theologian Rudolf Otto first coined this term to attempt to describe God's holiness.[1] He observed that God's holiness is not just "goodness," or merely a moral quality. We can see this from our text. The seraphim did not cry out, "Good, good, good is the LORD of hosts." Holiness is not just goodness, for goodness would never knock you dead, as holiness nearly did with Isaiah. The numinous is beyond expression; it eludes apprehension. It's raw and powerful, more than we could ever grasp. Otto also made it clear that numinous is more than the feeling of dependence. It's the emotion of being overwhelmed by your own nothingness before the throne of supreme power. He then went on to describe the *mysterium tremendum*, which is the way the human mind processes an encounter with the numinous. Mysterium tremendum is a feeling that comes from encountering the bewildering strength of God's holiness.

Otto defined *tremendum* as having elements of awefulness (tremors, fear, dread, awe); overpoweringness (majesty, might, power); and energy (urgency, passion, emotion). We see each of these in Isaiah 6. The prophet trembled in fear at the overpowering sight of God's glory. Next, Otto described *mysterium* as encountering "the wholly other." When this happens, you are left in a blank wonder, an astonishment that strikes us dumb. He said:

> The truly "mysterious" object is beyond our apprehension and comprehension, not only because our knowledge has certain irremovable limits, but because in it we come upon something inherently "wholly other," whose kind and character are incommensurable with our own, and before which we therefore recoil in a wonder that strikes us chill and numb.[2]

On the one hand, "our knowledge has certain irremovable limits." We are limited by our frame of dust and our soul of sin. We are not God, and there's nothing we can do about that. There are plenty of things in this world we can understand and even master. But we are infinitely out of our league when it comes to God. We have minimal capacity to comprehend the Divine. We have limits that can never be overcome. God's "kind and character" are so much more than ours. We are like a candle before a tornado, chill and numb.

Again, we see this in our text. The Lord was sitting on a throne, high and lifted up. This is a way of acknowledging that he is "wholly other." He is infinitely higher than us, on an entirely different level. We're told that the train of his robe filled the temple—just a small part of God could be seen. This is another way of saying that there's no way we can begin to understand or comprehend him. God is a mystery to us; we can merely comprehend some pieces on the bottom of his garment. We can never take in the full picture; to do so would be much too shocking.

Notice that the seraphim flew around with their faces covered. The word *seraphim* means "burning ones." They are fiery creatures whose wings give the impression of a blazing bonfire as they flap up and down in flight. Fire is the Bible's symbol for holiness, yet not even these flaming creatures could look upon the glory of God. God is "wholly other" than even the seraphim. Everything shook at the sound of God's voice, and the whole place filled with smoke, a symbol of God's presence. It adds to the mysterium tremendum. At the same time, it presents God and conceals God. It both draws us to God and drives us away from him, as our sinful souls choke on the smoke of his holiness.[3]

The seraphim cried out in ecstasy, "Holy, holy, holy is the LORD of hosts; the whole earth is full of his glory" (Isa. 6:3). Notice the shift from holiness to glory, as we go from the sacred throne room to the far corners of the earth. *Holiness is the superlative perfection and power of God's unapproachable being, while glory is that holiness put on display.* Glory is God's visible transcendence. Or, to use our idea from before, God's holiness is what we would experience onstage at Ravinia, while God's glory is what we would hear through the woods. God's holiness is the fountain from which his glory flows out into the world.

WHAT DOES GOD'S GLORY DO?

God's glory does at least two things when we come face-to-face with it. First, it convicts us of our sin; and second, it heals us. Or, as Otto put it, it causes both dread and delight. Here's the next part of the passage:

> And I said: "Woe is me! For I am lost; for I am a man of unclean lips, and I dwell in the midst of a people of unclean lips; for my eyes have seen the King, the LORD of hosts!"
>
> Then one of the seraphim flew to me, having in his hand a burning coal that he had taken with tongs from the altar. And he touched my mouth and said: "Behold, this has touched your lips; your guilt is taken away, and your sin atoned for." (Isa. 6:5–7)

Otto noted the dual aspects of God's glory as being both repulsive and fascinating. We tremble before it, yet we crave it. It scares us and lures us, like standing on the precipice of a cliff, comprehending both fear and inspiration. We're entranced and transported with a "strange ravishment."[4]

First, God's glory convicts us of our sin, but not just for the bad things we do. This is the nuanced version of the human predicament Isaiah offered. It's not just that human beings sin but that *we are sinners*. Isaiah was not being condemned for something he had done wrongly, but for whom he was at his best. Isaiah said, "Woe is me! For I am lost; for I am a man of unclean lips, and I dwell in the midst of a people of unclean lips." Isaiah wasn't confessing a foul mouth, responding in fear at having finally been caught. Rather, Isaiah was putting forth his greatest gift for examination. Isaiah was a prophet, so his mouth represented the best that he could offer God; yet, even his best feature would condemn him. God's glory shows us that it's not just our sin that we need to be afraid of but also our righteousness.

Isaiah said, "I am lost!" The Hebrew word for "lost" is the reaction that a dead person would give: *nothing*. God's glory knocked Isaiah as though dead; not even his righteousness could support his cause. He also acknowledged that his ethnic heritage couldn't save him. He came from a people with "unclean lips." Though the people of Israel had been set apart to reveal the oracles of God to the world, Isaiah couldn't rest on his ethnic laurels. Before God's glory, neither your good works nor your heritage can save you. The starting point of true spirituality is to admit that you are lost and can't do anything about it apart from God's grace. We're not just spiritually injured, but dead. It's as if a medieval castle has been dropped on us; we have no hope unless someone rescues us by taking our place.

Second, God's glory heals us. Can you imagine being in Isaiah's shoes? One of the burning ones, the seraphim, goes to the altar to pick up a burning coal, but his hand draws back, for the coals are too hot. He uses tongs to pick up the coal, and you realize how hot it must be if a creature made out of fire can't touch the surface. Then the seraphim starts to fly right toward your face with the burning coal! He touches one of the most tender parts of your body with the live ember. But it doesn't burn; instead, it heals. Somehow, the coal takes away your guilt and atones for your sin. The coal came from the altar, where the sacrifice would have been. No doubt blood from the sacrifice had dripped down onto the coals. The fire burned away your iniquities, leaving you pure. Until that moment, there was nothing you could do to make your guilt go away; now, for the first time ever, it is gone.

Just as this was a defining moment for Isaiah, it will be a defining moment for everyone who trembles before the numinous of God's holiness. It's the moment when we finally break through and realize that we're living in the midst of the most compelling performance of all time. When we finally realize that the echoes of the music all around us are coming from the stage of God's throne, we'll never see the world in the same way again. We'll never forget that picture of the seraphim, the house of smoke, the sacred robe, and the earthshaking voice. It's as if we've been drunk on the delusions of this world for so long and have suddenly been sobered by the reality of God. Only the Spirit can wake us up from our death sleep and remove our rotting grave clothes. His holiness is our alarm. God's glory lifts the crushing burden from our backs and sets us free.

But we don't want to be completely free from God's glory. That's how we know that we've truly been transformed: We begin to crave it. We want to enter into its story and live in its embrace. It terrifies us, but we can't stop seeking it out. We long to find that place of glorious trepidation again and again, experiencing the same fear and the same joy. We long to offer up our sins, over and over, and to feel them burned away every time. We long to live in the experience of God's presence and his mighty grace. We want to cry, and we want him to wipe away our tears. We want to possess the unpossessable and do whatever he wants. We don't want to go back to our old way of life, believing the same old lies and following the same meaningless pursuits. Having tasted living water, who could go back?

George Herbert wrote,

> Ah Lord! do not withdraw,
> Lest want of awe
> Make Sin appear ...[5]

Herbert recognized the human need for "awe." Our souls need to be awed by the holiness of God, for when they aren't, sin creeps closer. God's glory is the light that causes sin to scamper away like cockroaches to the corner. Those who don't experience awe before God are in danger of being overrun by the cares of this world. God's glory puts life back into proper perspective.

WHAT DOES GOD'S GLORY WANT?

God's glory wants to go from the throne to the ends of the earth on the lips of those who have encountered it. Isaiah 6:8–9 says:

> And I heard the voice of the Lord saying, "Whom shall I send, and who will go for us?" Then I said, "Here I am! Send me." And he said, "Go, and say to this people ..."

God's glory wants to make itself known to all the nations on earth so that everyone has a chance to repent (turn to God) and be healed. God's glory hates the darkness and wants to break it with its holy beams. It wants the whole world to see the King of Glory, who sits on the throne and offers forgiveness and reconciliation. Here's the vision Isaiah had of glory:

> Arise, shine, for your light has come,
>> and the glory of the LORD has risen upon you.
> For behold, darkness shall cover the earth,
>> and thick darkness the peoples;
> but the LORD will arise upon you,
>> and his glory will be seen upon you.
> And nations shall come to your light,
>> and kings to the brightness of your rising. (Isa.
>> 60:1–3)

Can you picture this magnificent scene? The darkness of hopelessness being shattered at last? The rule of suffering being overturned by the reign of joy? Can you see how God's glory wants to go to the ends of the earth? This is what our hearts have been longing for! The angels, whose faces were covered in Isaiah 6:2, have been eagerly awaiting the revelation of the mystery of God, which is Jesus Christ (1 Pet. 1:12). The message about Jesus is the good news that will finally break the darkness. It's the story of the incarnation of God, who entered into the darkness in order to ransom sinners from its clutches. Ironically, Jesus's death on the cross was the most staggering manifestation of God's glory. It traveled from the throne to the cross, where it shined the brightest. Jesus on the cross is the blood-soaked live coal. In heaven, God's glory looks one way; on earth, it looks another. Before both, sinners tremble.

But how will the message of Jesus get to the ends of the earth? God's glory chooses to travel from person to person. Recall the garden of Eden, where one lie traveled from creature to creature. The serpent passed the lie to Eve, and then Eve passed the lie to Adam. The world was condemned through sin that spread one person at a time. In the same way, God's glory chooses to travel from person to person. Just as God asked one person, Isaiah, to step forward, so does God ask us to step forward to carry his glory to the ends of the earth. "Whom shall I send?" Send me! God chooses the instrument of the human voice to spread his glory throughout the world. We are his bullets and bombs against the enemy, as we share the story of Jesus Christ, who is the glory of God. This is not just our purpose but the only reasonable response after encountering the numinous.[6]

But it won't be easy. God told Isaiah that the people he would speak with wouldn't understand his message. "Keep on hearing, but do not understand; keep on seeing, but do not perceive" (Isa. 6:9). No one ever said that it would be easy to be a Christian and spread the message about Jesus Christ. As it was for Isaiah, so will it be for us. But what do we expect? Remember, to encounter the glory of God is to be permanently changed; you can't go back to how you were before.

LEAVE THE OLD LIFE BEHIND

If you follow Jesus, your life will start heading in a different direction—the direction of his choosing. Like someone who gets a tattoo, the follower of Jesus must be bold, decisive, and willing to change.

It's all or nothing. One has to be willing to let go of the person she was before if she is going to follow Jesus. She must be willing to change her life permanently if she is going to commit to him. There's no such thing as a Christian who doesn't lose her old life in order to gain her new one. But don't feel sorry for her, because she traded in a few coins for an eternal inheritance.

The last chapter of the book of Acts picks up on an idea that's critical for us to understand, especially as it relates to Isaiah's frustrations with speaking God's word to his people, elaborated on in Isaiah 6:9–13. In Acts 28, the mighty apostle Paul was sitting in a prison, chained to a guard. We don't want his story to end this way, but we might be disappointed. If we trace Paul's story from Acts 9 on the Damascus Road in Israel all the way to Rome in Acts 28, we learn that Paul overcame obstacle after obstacle: arguments, mobs, riots, jail, beatings, shipwrecks, plots, death threats, storms, hunger, and thirst. It seemed like nothing could stop him.

Every time I read the book of Acts, I'm always disappointed when I get to the end. I want there to be an Acts 29, a better ending to his story. Here's how I want it to end: "With the help of an angel, Paul escaped from the Roman guard. He made it all the way back home to Jerusalem. He entered the home of Peter, everybody gave high fives, and Paul told the riveting account of his miraculous escape. Then they ate some fish." But there is no Acts 29. The story ends with Paul sitting in prison, soberly reflecting on Isaiah 6:9–10.

> Go to this people, and say,
> "You will indeed hear but never understand,

and you will indeed see but never perceive."
For this people's heart has grown dull,
    and with their ears they can barely hear,
    and their eyes they have closed;
lest they should see with their eyes
    and hear with their ears
and understand with their heart
    and turn, and I would heal them.
        (Acts 28:26–27)

Do you know the difference between a quest and an adventure? An adventure is an exciting journey, a daring or dangerous undertaking, which is often unusual or stirring. But at the end of the day, you come home, back to your old life. You return to the shore from which you first departed. The person who is seeking adventure will experience thrills, have something to tell others about, and might even risk his life. But the goal of an adventure is to return home. The person who is going on a quest, on the other hand, sets off in pursuit of something. A quest is a journey in pursuit of a goal. It's linear, not circular. There is no expectation of returning to the starting point. The person on a quest doesn't care if he ever returns to the shore from which he departed. In fact, the person who is on a quest might never attain what he is looking for, dying in breathless pursuit of it. But more importantly, he doesn't expect ever to be the same, because he isn't after momentary thrills, but something worth dying for. Come what may, he is committed to the mission.

Paul was on a quest, not an adventure. He didn't follow Jesus for momentary thrills or to gather exciting stories to tell others. He didn't become a follower of Jesus with the expectation of remaining the same. He knew Jesus would lead him to new horizons. Think about Paul's journey, from Jerusalem to Rome, from starting off as a zealous Jew to dying as a Christian martyr. His life was a quest. His goal was to bring the word of God about Jesus Christ to the nations. In the beginning of Acts, God had already mentioned his program to the church.[7] In Acts 1:8, Jesus said to his first followers, "But you will receive power when the Holy Spirit has come upon you, and you will be my witnesses in Jerusalem and in all Judea and Samaria, and to the end of the earth." Though Paul wasn't there when Jesus spoke these words, he was enlisted by Jesus in Acts 9:15–16 for this mission. Viewed this way, the last chapter of Acts isn't a downer, but a note of triumph. Paul was at "the end of the earth" in Rome, chained to a Gentile (the Roman guard), proclaiming the message of Jesus Christ. As the last word of the book of Acts says, Paul's life was "unhindered."[8]

Or consider the vow Ruth made to Naomi. After Naomi's husband and two sons died, she was alone. She expected her daughters-in-law to leave her and go back to their old lives. Though one of them did, the other did not. Ruth said to her mother-in-law:

> Do not urge me to leave you or to return from fol-
> lowing you. For where you go I will go, and where
> you lodge I will lodge. Your people shall be my
> people, and your God my God. Where you die I
> will die, and there will I be buried. May the LORD
> do so to me and more also if anything but death
> parts me from you. (Ruth 1:16–17)

Because of her commitment to her mother-in-law, Ruth realized that her life would never be the same. Everything would change: her home, people, and religion. Ruth's life was a quest, not an adventure. She knew that holding on to her old life would hinder her quest to remain loyal.

I have found this immensely helpful in my understanding of the Christian life. A Christian is someone who is on a quest, not an adventure. A Christian knows that the kind of person she is when she embarks is not the kind of person she'll be ten years into the journey. The Christian leaves her old life on one shore and places all of her hopes and dreams on another shore—one she can't yet see when she climbs into the boat. The Christian can say with Ruth, "Where you go I will go." God isn't leading us on daily adventures just to keep life interesting, but on a quest to spread his glory.

Are you disappointed that life has changed? Do you want to go back to the way things were? God has not led you this far in order for you to turn back now. There is more ocean to swim. There is more for you to do, more places for you to spread God's glory. There are dark places and unreached places, both in your life and in the lives of others. These are places that are waiting to hear from someone who has encountered the glory of God and been shaken by it. This is your quest.

Think about the kinds of things that Jesus taught. "If your right eye causes you to sin, tear it out and throw it away.... If your right hand causes you to sin, cut it off and throw it away." "Whoever loves father or mother more than me is not worthy of me, and whoever loves son or daughter more than me is not worthy of me. And whoever does not take his cross and follow me is not worthy of me"

(Matt. 5:29–30; 10:37–38). Does it sound like Jesus has in mind an adventure or a quest? Jesus's words are decisive because he has in mind life change. Jesus doesn't want us to go back. He doesn't call us to live basically the same life, with some spiritual highs thrown in on Sunday mornings. He's leading us on a greater, deeper quest. We're headed to another shore, and it's okay if we never return to where we were before or the way we were before. There is no such thing as a Christian who returns each night to the shore from which he left just to go out again the next day unchanged. That's insanity. The Christian life is not just a safe addition to our own lives but a total overhaul.

Consider the gravitational pull of the stars, moon, and planets. Objects are sucked into these celestial bodies. The heavier the body, the greater the gravity. This is a good way of understanding God's glory, which contains hints of "weight" in its meaning. The more we experience the glory of God, the more we're drawn in by the grip of gravity. The greater our sense of "awe" before the holiness of God, the more the course of our lives will change so that we're no longer drawn in by smaller things, but by God. We no longer want to return to our old course, because we're compelled by the weight of heaven. Just as the apostle Peter leaped from the boat to swim to Jesus, so will we leap from our old lives in order to swim to the shore where he stands (John 21).

God says to us, "I created you for my glory." That is both our purpose and our mission. We are to spread the glory of God to the ends of the earth. It all starts when we are permanently changed by an encounter with God, the mysterium tremendum. When this happens, our self-orbit is broken. The old theological saying *homo incurvatus in se* teaches us that humans are bent in on themselves in a deadly spiral. Though we were meant to orbit God and receive life from him, we chose to leave a universe with him at the center, all but sealing our fate. Only an encounter with the glory of God can snap our necks straight again. Then we'll be able to hold our heads high and move out for God and for others. When Moses encountered the glory of God, it "landed" on his face so that others could see it shining brightly (Exod. 34:29). In the same way, so will our encounter with God's glory be a light to others. Isaiah was baptized in God's holiness, and he "died" beneath its electric waters, only to be raised by the power of atonement. We have been baptized into Christ Jesus, who has freed us from sin to live for the glory of God.

CHAPTER 11

THE NAME ON
YOUR ARM

Fear not, for I am with you; I will bring your
offspring from the east, and from the west I will
gather you. I will say to the north, Give up, and
to the south, Do not withhold; bring my sons
from afar and my daughters from the end of the
earth, everyone who is called by my name, whom I
created for my glory, whom I formed and made.

Isaiah 43:5–7

LOST

Have you ever considered the searching questions humans ask? Surely you're familiar with two of the most common, "Who am I?" and "Why am I here?" At first glance, these kinds of questions appear deep and penetrating. They remind me of the sort of question you might find on a college philosophy exam. In reality, however, these questions are quite basic, so long as you don't overthink them.

Ask a child these questions and you'll get confident responses. Who am I? "I'm Andrew." Why am I here? "I'm here for lunch," or whatever the case may be. Ask a football player the same questions and you'll hear a similar tone of confidence. Who am I? "I'm a quarterback." Why am I here? "I'm here to win the football game!" Do you see what I mean? These two seemingly profound questions are really quite basic. Everyone should be able to answer them. Unless, of course, you're not where you were meant to be.

Imagine if you could travel back in time to the year 1714 and kidnap an English princess. You send her to the future and place her in an F-18 Hornet during the middle of a raging air battle. What sort of questions is she most likely to ask? "Who am I?" and "Why am I here?" We know from experience that we typically ask these questions when we're lost or misplaced. Or think about a child who loses his parents. Only when he is lost does he begin to ask these searching questions, because he wants to be found.

Questions like these betray the fundamental reality that we're far from our true home. Our first home was the garden of Eden, where we dwelled with God. Were we in the garden today, we would never ask, "Who am I?" and "Why am I here?" *In the direct presence of God, it would be obvious.* There would be nothing left to wonder. Only because we have been exiled from the garden, our true home, do we ask these questions.

EVICTION

God's people are lost. They aren't at home with God but are scattered to the four corners of the compass, to the west, east, north, and south. How did they get so far from home? They were evicted because of their disobedience. The original eviction was in the garden of Eden, where God pronounced both eviction and death because of disobedience (Gen. 3:23–24). Since then, God's people have been struggling to make it back home. They spent four hundred years in Egypt, forty years in the wilderness, and nearly seventy years in Babylon. They made a ruin of their lives, coughing up God's blessings for the sake of false securities. Any time we trust in idols to save us, we do the same.

Whenever you're evicted, you lose something precious. When Adam and Eve were evicted from the garden, they lost life and blessing. When the people of Israel were evicted to Egypt, they lost their freedom. When they were evicted to Babylon, they lost their treasures and possessions (2 Chron. 36:18–20), as well as the presence of God (Ezek. 10). This is how we've been ruined.

But even though God's people were far from him, both geographically and spiritually, they possessed a fundamental marker of hope. They had a calling and an identity that assured their restoration. They were called by the name of the Lord, and they had been made for his glory. It was as if they had the name of the Lord tattooed on their arms. Though they often felt afraid, they had nothing to be afraid of.

> Fear not, for I am with you; I will bring your offspring from the east, and from the west I will gather you. I will say to the north, Give up, and to the south, Do not withhold; bring my sons from afar and my daughters from the end of the earth, everyone who is called by my name, whom I created for my glory, whom I formed and made. (Isa. 43:5–7)

With just one primeval shout, the four corners of the earth would be forced to bow and surrender their captives. Eviction would be the new road home.

There is a tattoo on your soul that says, "You were created for my glory." This is a homing device that has already been activated, despite your eviction. It was activated by the one who was sent to save us. This tattoo throbs with promise.

By now, you know that Jesus saved us on the cross when he died for our sins. But there's much more to explore here. In order for us to understand fully what it means to be created for God's glory, we have to understand Jesus's narrative. Once we understand Jesus's narrative, we'll be able to understand our own. Then we'll see how the soul tattoo "I created you for my glory" fills us with hope and joy.

THE STORY BEHIND THE STORY

The story of Jesus has to do with his life, death, and resurrection, parts of which we have explored. But there's a story *behind* the story. We learn about it from another passage of Scripture.

> Have this mind among yourselves, which is yours
> in Christ Jesus, who, though he was in the form of
> God, did not count equality with God a thing to be
> grasped, but emptied himself, by taking the form of
> a servant, being born in the likeness of men. And
> being found in human form, he humbled himself
> by becoming obedient to the point of death, even
> death on a cross. Therefore God has highly exalted

him and bestowed on him the name that is above
every name, so that at the name of Jesus every knee
should bow, in heaven and on earth and under the
earth, and every tongue confess that Jesus Christ is
Lord, to the glory of God the Father. (Phil. 2:5–11)

Here we learn about the two movements of Jesus's life, which
form the plot of the story behind the story. First, we discover that
Jesus was evicted. The text tells us that at one point, Jesus shared
"equality with God." He was at home with God. But he decided to
empty himself of that equality and enter into exile. After emptying
himself, he went further, taking on the form of a servant. His descend-
ing didn't stop there, for he didn't just become a lowly human, but
he went all the way down to death. It says that he became "obedient" to death, as if it became his master. This is staggering when you
consider the height from which he came. The Master of all became
the Slave of all. And it's not just that he submitted to death but to
"death on a cross." This proves his ultimate eviction, calling upon
the ancient curse of Deuteronomy 21:23, which says, "A hanged [on
a tree] man is cursed by God." Jesus didn't submit just to death but
also to our curse. That's as low as anyone could go and as far from
God as possible. That's the first half of the story.

The second half of the story is found in Philippians 2:9–11.
"Therefore God has highly exalted him and bestowed on him the
name that is above every name." From the cursed grave, Jesus began
to rise. He didn't just return from the grave, though that would have
been spectacular enough; he went further. He rose past the grave,
past the earth, and all the way to the throne of God. "So that at the

name of Jesus every knee should bow, in heaven and on earth and under the earth." He became the ruler of all rulers, before whom all knees tremble, "and every tongue confess that Jesus Christ is Lord." The second half of the story is his ascension to the throne, where he became the King of Kings "to the *glory* of God the Father." Note how *eviction* in Philippians 2:5–8 leads to *glory* in Philippians 2:9–11.

That's the story behind the story, Jesus's exile and return. You could also call it his eviction and coronation. I like imagining it as *the voyage of Christ, from ruin to reign.* Now can you see how Jesus has begun to map his life onto ours? Just as we ruined our lives, he ruined his life in order to meet us and identify with us. Our ruin was met by his, but his went further, as he descended to the cursed pit of total abandonment by God, where no human has ever been. Just as Jacob stole his brother's birthright, so did Jesus steal our curse—but he left his birthright to us. This birthright gives us the right to reign.

Our Savior was launched from heaven. He set off on a voyage to rescue us, to match our exile in every way, even to the point of being laid on wood, activating the ancient curse that was meant for us. He became lost, crying out as a missing child, searching for his Father, "Why have you forsaken me?" (Matt. 27:46). He had to become lost because we were lost. He left his home, because we had left our home.

OUR NEXT CHAPTER

In order to figure out the next chapter of our lives, we have to study and understand the story behind the story of Jesus's life, from ruin to reign. Where does the plot go from here for us? We've been evicted, so according to Jesus's narrative, the chapters of our restoration come next. Because Jesus took the curse, we pass over the chapter of death and enter into the chapter of life. We skip the chapter about the curse and can go directly to homecoming.

Keeping in mind the voyage of Jesus, from ruin to reign, we're now able to understand our last soul tattoo, "I created you for my glory." Just as Jesus's two-part story ended in the glory of God, so will ours. "I created you for my glory" summarizes where we are headed. Just as Jesus went from ruin to reign, so will you and I.

We, too, have a story behind the story. On the one hand, we have the story of our lives; you have yours and I have mine. I was born in Ohio, in a family of seven, went to college, got married, and so forth. You have a story too. That story is important, but it's not *fundamental*. The fundamental story of my life is the story of ruin and reign, summarized by the soul tattoo "I created you for my glory." We often get caught up in our own little stories; actually, that's not strong enough: we get *swallowed up* in our own stories. Surrounded by the stomachs of our stories, we're consumed by their deadly juices, and hope is digested away. However, those who trust in Jesus have an unkillable backbone, a story behind the story, which nothing can destroy.

This soul tattoo is a homing device. Upon its activation, we are pointed home and pulled there by the gravity of God's love, no matter where we once were. Its mere presence reveals to us the second half of our story, which erupts out of the ruin. "I created you for my glory" teaches us that we were meant to reign. Our downward trajectory also contains an upward one. With this background knowledge, we can now understand the excitement swirling around these verses in Isaiah 43:5–7. Their utterance means that the countdown to launch has begun. While we don't know how long the countdown will be, we do know that the engines have been switched on. We look at the title of the next chapter of our lives—*"I created you for my glory"*—and we know exactly where we're headed.

THE SPIRIT'S ACTIVITY

But how do we get there? We know all too well our lost and ruined state, but how do we get to our reigning state? To be created for God's glory seems like an incredible, if not impossible, task to live up to. We understand how Jesus could live "to the glory of God the Father" (Phil. 2:11), but *us*? How will our ruin lead to glory, as his did (in Philippians 2)?

The answer can be found in Romans 8, where we learn about the ministry of the Holy Spirit. The Holy Spirit seeks to map us into the likeness of Jesus Christ.[1] Just as Jesus matched our state of ruin, the Spirit is seeking to match us to his state of reigning. Jesus was sent "in the likeness of sinful flesh and for sin" (v. 3). The Spirit was sent so that we might be "conformed to the image of his Son" (v. 29). Right away, you can see the familiar story behind the story: "For I consider that the sufferings of this present time are not worth comparing with the glory that is to be revealed to us" (v. 18). We see both our ruin ("the sufferings of this present time") and our future reign ("the glory that is to be revealed to us"). The Bible longs for the day when "we may also be glorified with him [Jesus]" (v. 17). Before we look at the specific activity of the Spirit in Romans 8, here is a summary statement that again captures the story of eviction and exaltation:

If the Spirit of him who raised Jesus from the dead
dwells in you, he who raised Christ Jesus from
the dead will also give life to your mortal bodies
through his Spirit who dwells in you. (v. 11)

The same Spirit who raised Jesus from ruin to reign will also
raise us from ruin to reign! The Spirit sets us free from the law of sin
and death (Rom. 8:2). Sin and death won't have the last word on
your life. The Spirit connects us to Jesus, the one who fulfilled all the
righteous requirements of the law for us (v. 4). The Spirit gives us life
and peace (v. 6). The Spirit helps us to live lives that are pleasing to
God (v. 8). The Spirit will give life to our mortal bodies (v. 11). The
Spirit gives us the power to put to death the evil deeds of the flesh (v.
13). The Spirit brings us out of fear (v. 15). The Spirit adopts us into
God's family so that we can call him our Father (v. 15). The Spirit
reminds us that we are children of God (v. 16). The Spirit makes us
into fellow heirs with Jesus Christ (v. 17). The Spirit will redeem our
bodies (v. 23). The Spirit gives us hope and helps us to wait with
patience (vv. 24–25). The Spirit helps us in our weakness (v. 26). The
Spirit helps us to pray when we don't know what to say (v. 26). The
Spirit intercedes for us, praying on our behalf with true unction and
according to the Father's perfect will (vv. 26–27). The Spirit searches
our hearts and helps us to know God's will (v. 27). The Spirit works
all things together for good (v. 28).

Not only is your soul tattoo "I created you for my glory" a homing device, but it is also a portrait of what the Spirit of God is making
you to be. He is mapping you into someone who is more than a conqueror (Rom. 8:37). Here's an appropriate summary from another of

Paul's letters: "If we have died with him, we will also live with him; if
we endure, we will also reign with him" (2 Tim. 2:11–12).

FAITH LIKE TATTOOS

"Who am I?" You are one of God's children who will reign with
his Son, even as you are being mapped into his likeness. "Why am
I here?" You are here to live for the glory of God. But how do we
live for the glory of God? *By believing his promises.* I'm not talking
about token belief: "God, I'll give you my trust in exchange for all
the riches of heaven." It's not like playing Go Fish. I'm talking about
robust, aching, do-or-die belief; the kind that's as tough as tattoos.
By now, you have a good grasp on these four promises of God: *you
are mine, I will be with you, I love you,* and *I created you for my glory.*
Now it's time to rise from the ruins by the power of the Holy Spirit
and trust in them. It's time to be like Abraham, who believed against
all odds:

> In the presence of the God in whom he believed,
> who gives life to the dead and calls into existence
> the things that do not exist. In hope he believed
> against hope, that he should become the father of
> many nations, as he had been told.… He did not
> weaken in faith when he considered his own body,
> which was as good as dead (since he was about a
> hundred years old), or when he considered the bar-
> renness of Sarah's womb. No unbelief made him
> waver concerning the promise of God, but he grew

strong in his faith as he gave glory to God, fully
convinced that God was able to do what he had
promised. (Rom. 4:17–21)

Everything was stacked against Abraham; he had no logical reason to trust God's promises. This is the kind of faith God calls us to,
the kind that requires supreme effort. It won't be easy. You will be
called to believe against all odds, when the promises seem as good as
dead. Notice the repetition of the "death" idea in these verses. We're
told God gives "life to the dead." We're told that Abraham's body
was "as good as dead." We're told that Sarah's womb was dead. But
against these staggering odds of death, Abraham believed in life. He
believed in a God who gives "life to the dead." By juxtaposing death
with life so many times, God is pointing our eyes to the resurrection.
He wants us to see and know that true faith ultimately believes in the
resurrection of Jesus Christ. Tattoo faith looks to the resurrection as
the justification for belief and hope.

Believing that God brings life out of death is the strongest expression of faith we can show. When we show this kind of indelible faith,
we give glory to God, fulfilling our purpose. "He grew strong in his
faith as he gave glory to God." Belief in God's promise to restore life
is not for the faint of heart or for the weak. It is for those who believe
that the tattoos on their souls speak louder than their scars.

ZION

It's like the faith of my friend Josh and his wife, Robbyn. I've known
Josh for a number of years now. I've seen his faith endure several

abrasive circumstances, such as changes in employment, a flooded house, and children in the ER. Josh is an excellent musician, and I've seen him use his musical gift at many concerts, events, and church services. I've watched him carry his guitar into church dozens of times, always with a smile, in an act of praise. As a friend, I admit that I've always taken his faith for granted.

But I'll never forget when I saw him display Abrahamic faith, the kind that only God can map onto you. He and his wife lost their son, Zion Isaiah. Little Zion died just ten days after he was born. The funeral was heartrending.

I've been to many funerals, and I know what to expect. After the service, the bereaved family stands up and walks out with the coffin, which is usually carried by the pallbearers. I fully expected to see the pallbearers escort Zion from the church, just as I'm used to. So when Josh came down the aisle all by himself carrying his son in the casket, his family trailing behind, it jolted me. I had seen Josh carry many things *into* a church before, but I had never seen him carrying such a weight as this *out* of a church before. I immediately thought of Job, who said, "The LORD gave, and the LORD has taken away; blessed be the name of the LORD" (Job 1:21). Josh wasn't about to let anyone else carry his precious Zion for this last time.

Then I thought of Abraham, whom God called to surrender his own son, Isaac. Genesis 22 tells us that Abraham didn't withhold his only son from God, demonstrating his unwavering faith in God. As I saw my friend carrying out his son in a little box, I felt I was watching Abraham. I was witnessing the miracle of tattoo faith.

At the end of a video honoring Zion's all-too-brief life, which was played at the funeral, Josh's voice came on, saying, "See you soon, son." They believed in the resurrection, which would bring life from death. Despite the tragedy, Josh and Robbyn maintain hope in the promises of God. Robbyn says that the verse she has held on to during this difficult time is Hebrews 6:19, which says, "We have this hope as an anchor for the soul" (NIV). Or, it could be said of them, "They grew strong in their faith as they gave glory to God."

They had chosen the name Zion because of Psalm 50:2, which says, "Out of Zion, the perfection of beauty, God shines forth." What a perfect name. Our faith in God shines forth his glory. Josh and Robbyn's faith challenges me to exert unwavering faith in God's promises. Our soul tattoos aren't there just for decoration but also for declaration. "I created you for my glory."

PERFORM THE PROMISES

My family and I went to the community theater to see a musical production. Partway through the show, during one of the song-and-dance routines, a resilient little girl came out onstage in a wheelchair. By the look of her legs, it was clear she had never walked before. She was about ten years old. There was another person behind her, pushing the chair according to the choreography of the routine. The young woman behind the chair escorted the girl to every corner of the stage. She zipped confidently around, allowing this precious, disabled girl to play an important role in the performance. Since the girl couldn't use her legs to perform the kicks that the dance required, she waved her arms back and forth instead. Her timing wasn't perfect, *but she was.* Her wheelchair was decorated in costume so that she matched the other dancers. She and the woman pushing the chair looped and swirled around the stage, maneuvering around the dozens of other dancers, holding their place with terrific poise. While the entire performance was wonderful, the audience was rapt by the girl in the wheelchair. We erupted in applause after her first routine. I had to fight back tears.

When I remember this little girl, I can't help but think about our faith. We, too, have a Helper, the Holy Spirit, who enables us to do what we could never do on our own. We, too, are on a stage performing. Our stage is the place where we live, and our performance is living out our faith in the promises of God. It's not easy, especially because we are disabled, broken. But we're called to perform to the glory of God, the one who has written the script and choreographed our movements. He knows our position on the stage, our lines, where we've been, and where we're headed. He puts us in routines that stretch us and spin us, but his Helper will never leave us. He will keep pushing us further into the drama, presenting us before the watchful eyes of the world.

Your soul tattoo reads "I created you for my glory." Speak with confidence the lines that show trust in the promises of God. Don't let brokenness keep you out of the show. The Spirit of God will guide you in Jesus's footsteps and map your movements according to his. This is our living performance, which we practice each day of our lives, in anticipation of when we'll perform it before the throne of God, on unbroken legs.

AFTER CARE

If you get a skin tattoo, your artist will provide you with crucial after-care instructions. The competent and caring artist will let you know how vital it is to adhere to these important guidelines, for even a beautiful tattoo can turn disastrous if it isn't taken care of properly. For instance, right after you get a tattoo, you must leave the bandage on it for two hours. Don't submerge it in water for two weeks. And for the rest of your life, put at least SPF 30 sunscreen on it before exposing it to sunlight so that the colors do not fade.

If taking care of our bodies is this important, how much more important is it to take care of our souls? I'm not saying that our soul tattoos will fade and become infected like a skin tattoo might, but I'm underscoring the importance of taking care of our souls. God won't erase the tattoos he has engraved on the souls of those who trust in him. They will remain for eternity. However, there are guidelines we can follow in order to maintain the vitality of our souls. Here are five ways to care for your soul tattoos, followed by six typical ways in which Satan attacks us.

BIBLE

You must read the Bible, both for information and for nourishment. Your soul depends on the truths found in the Bible. There's no way around this. You and I need to have a daily diet of Bible reading. On one level, reading the Bible is like exercising: While you can't always feel its positive effects, you can trust that it's changing you. Even if you don't feel like going for a jog or lifting weights, doing so will still benefit your body. The Bible isn't like other books, for when you use it as exercise for your soul, your soul is strengthened. It's more like ink than water, leaving its mark on those who come into contact with it.

Some might say, "But I read the Bible, and I know its stories. I think it's boring!" In response, we might ask, "Did you eat breakfast this morning? Didn't you have breakfast yesterday? Why did you have to eat it again today? Isn't breakfast boring?" We don't eat breakfast because it's particularly thrilling, but because it keeps us alive and nourished. Some of the most vital things in our lives are also the most "boring." There's nothing much more boring than breathing! Yet, without it, we'll die. The same is true of the Bible: without it, our souls will die.

Thankfully, it's not boring! To read the Bible with an open heart is to encounter an extraordinary portrait of Jesus Christ. From beginning to end, the Bible is a display of Jesus, in all his beauty, wisdom, power, and steadfast love. All the stories in the Bible point to Jesus. If you're ever uncertain about the meaning of a passage of Scripture, filter it through this grid: our problem, God's solution, and our response. Ask yourself what human problem is presented in the story, discover God's solution to that problem, and search for an appropriate response to God's solution. Here's a hint: God's ultimate solution to every human problem is Jesus Christ. Here's one more practical tip: Don't skip a day of Bible reading (just as you normally wouldn't skip a day of eating), and don't skim through the stories. Read through one book of the Bible at a time, from start to finish.[1]

PRAYER

Prayer goes hand in hand with Bible reading. The Bible teaches us what to pray about. Try to keep these two together as much as possible. My motto is "Bible reading isn't complete without prayer; prayer can't begin without Bible reading." During prayer, the Holy Spirit works in at least three ways. First, the Spirit teaches us more about God and what we learned from his Word while reading. Second, the Spirit carries our prayers before the throne and intercedes on our behalf. Third, the Spirit is sent from the throne to grant certain requests on earth, according to God's sovereign plan.

When we pray, we "visit our true home" in heaven for a few thrilling moments while we're still on earth. God uses prayer as a way to comfort us, remind us of the truth, and give us divine wisdom. Prayer is a way of experiencing your relationship with God. Prayer draws our attention to our soul tattoos: "You are mine," "I will be with you," "I love you," and "I created you for my glory."

We must be careful that we don't try to manipulate God with our prayers, either by making ourselves look "good," bargaining, or commanding. God is our loving and faithful heavenly Father; he knows us inside and out, and he knows what we need. Finally, talk to him with this in mind: that you will one day see Jesus Christ and you will one day be like him (1 John 3:2). By keeping these truths in mind, you will filter out hopelessness on the one hand and pride on the other. Pray for big things and for small things, because God loves it when his children depend on him!

WORSHIP

Your soul also needs to worship God in order to be healthy. Remember the gravitational pull? The more mass an object has, the more gravitational pull it will exert. Our souls will orbit around the things in our lives that have the greatest weight or mass. If God is the biggest thing in your life, your heart will orbit around him. Think about the things you struggle with, such as pride, lust, or doubt. Why is this the case? Because we've put something else at our center; we've allowed something else to be bigger than God, so it has more "pull" on our souls.

When we read the Bible and pray, we learn more about our Creator. He gets "heavier" in our lives. In response, we worship. To worship is to put God at the center of our lives and make him bigger than any other thing. We aren't called to forget about our problems during worship, but we are to place them next to God (though not at the center) and discover how much greater he is than our problems.

While worship can come in many forms, such as singing, serving, giving, working, creating, or learning, the outcome of worship is the same. To worship is to seek him intentionally with every part of you.

COMMUNITY

Your soul needs other Christians in order to be healthy. The church might be flawed, but it's the body of Christ (Rom. 12:3–8). Just as the body contains many members, so does your soul. It's not just "you and Jesus." It's the church and Jesus, for he is the head of the church. When we're in community, we best reflect God and experience God, who exists as Father, Son, and Holy Spirit. We're also stronger when we're together. While it's easy to break a single arrow, it's virtually impossible to break a bundle of arrows. Our faith is made stronger when bundled together in the body of Christ. Community is where we learn about covenant relationship and what it means to commit to others out of a heart of service.

Find a local church that faithfully teaches the Bible and is full of grace, and walk boldly into community. Look for ways you can serve in the church, be mentored by others in the church, and be served by the church. Community is a wonderful place to be reminded of our soul tattoos.

OUTREACH

Outreach must be a part of our daily lives in order for our souls to be healthy. What is outreach? It is serving those around us. We serve by caring for the physical, emotional, social, and spiritual needs of others. Don't miss the implications here. Though physical needs surely are the most obvious, we fail in outreach if we don't also care for spiritual needs. It would make little sense to give someone a glass of water one minute if you knew that his whole ship would sink in five. If the physical needs of this world are many—and they are—how much greater are its spiritual needs? To do outreach work is to join Jesus Christ in his mission to establish the kingdom of heaven on earth.

GUARD AGAINST THESE ATTACKS FROM SATAN

There is a spiritual being who has placed a target on you. He is the adversary of those who follow Jesus Christ, and he aims his poisonous darts at you. Did you struggle through any of the previous chapters, wrestling with doubt or unbelief? That's Satan's work. He loves to keep us from living out the reality of our soul tattoos. Though he has many strategies for attacking us, I would like to share six of them. Just as bacteria seek to infect our bodies, so does Satan seek to infect and take over our souls.

LIES

Satan will lie to you in order to keep you from realizing the incredible promises of God. He will tell you that you aren't accepted, can't be forgiven, aren't worth it, are all alone, and can never be good enough. Have you heard these lies? Sound familiar? With these lies, he will seek to rip a hole in your soul through which all of God's promises will drain. The only way to fight his lies is with the truth, which will repair the damage. Remember your soul tattoos, and fight against his wicked taunts.

LAZINESS

Satan also seeks to stoke laziness in our lives. He will convince us that it's not necessary to seek God or put him first. He will call this "silliness." He will constantly point out the path of least resistance and try to convince us that this is God's will, since it's easiest. Satan loves it when our souls are fat and sleepy from the pleasures of this world. He tries to put time on our hands so that we become idle; the less we have to do, the more we tend to focus on ourselves. Scum forms on the top of stagnant water, not running water.

SELF-SUFFICIENCY

Self-sufficiency keeps us from depending on God and others. Because of our pride, we want to be more important than others. This causes us to focus on appearances—on looking good rather than genuinely serving those around us according to how God has made us and with the gifts he has given us. Not only does pride keep us from joy, but also it tightens Satan's rope around us. Pride is the name of Satan's leash, which he uses to lead us away from God.

A CRITICAL SPIRIT

One of Satan's favorite tactics is to point out all the problems of the church. Have you ever noticed that we're far more critical when it comes to the church than with other groups? We'll look past the short-comings of a club, a professional organization, or friends at the local bar, but we'll not let one misdeed of a church member go unnoticed. We'll grab hold of it and lift it up as our excuse for not committing. The honest person will admit that he has double standards. "But it's not supposed to be like that in the church!" we say. "The church is supposed to be different from other groups!" we contest. The church is comprised of sinners who are saved by grace, not social skills. We need to have realistic expectations, for there are no perfect churches. Satan tries to convince us that the church must be perfect or it's unworthy of our attention. He'll appeal to our pride and say things like "You deserve better than that. Look at those hypocrites! You're not like that." Satan wants us to believe that the church is a lost cause. Ever wonder why he's so intent on making it appear this way? The church of Jesus Christ is what Satan fears the most. So stick to it, be committed to a community, and keep making Satan nervous.

EXCUSES

Have you ever noticed that it's often easier to read a novel or a biography than it is to read the Bible? We claim that the Bible is too hard to understand, and we formulate dozens of excuses why we can't read it. Satan lurks behind every attempt to read the Bible. The father of lies hates it when we're exposed to the truth. He will do everything in his power to keep us from exercising our souls with Scripture: sleepiness, confusion, apathy, busyness, or snobbery. Sometimes we impose a double standard when it comes to our younger church members. We'll excuse the lack of deep study by saying, "They're just students. Don't teach them theology or expect them to know the Bible." But in school, the same students learn physics, geometry, Chinese, microbiology, computer science, calculus, poetry, linguistics, Latin, and more! Surely they can learn the definition of justification with just as much ease.

HOPELESSNESS

Faith is the glue that connects us to God. Satan seeks to dissolve that glue so we don't experience God's power. Satan will convince us that

our sins are too powerful and that we can't overcome them. He will
argue that our situation is hopeless and beyond repair. He will settle
it in our hearts that we are too weak and pathetic to be of much use
to God. But God is more powerful than our sins, all of life ends in
glory, and the Holy Spirit provides us with the power to overcome.
Though Satan wants us to shrink back and give up, we must reach
out and grab hold of God's power.

We don't follow these guidelines in order to earn God's favor; we
follow them to take care of the gift God has already given to us. Being
a Christian isn't easy, and our souls have many enemies. But now that
you have these soul tattoos, you can reenter your life with irrevocable
hope, for you have stains that run much deeper than scars.

NOTES

THE PARLOR CHAIR IS OPEN

1. "Tattooed Gen Nexters," Pew Research Center, www.pewresearch
.org/daily-number/tattooed-gen-nexters/.
2. Bonnie Berkowitz, "Tattooing Outgrows Its Renegade Image to
Thrive in the Mainstream," *Washington Post*, February 8, 2011,
www.washingtonpost.com/wp-dyn/content/article/2011/02/07/
AR2011020704915.html.
3. Laura Hillenbrand, *Unbroken: A World War II Story of Survival,
Resilience and Redemption* (New York: Random, 2010), 182–83.
4. Hillenbrand, *Unbroken*, 183.
5. Coldplay, "Fix You," *X&Y*, Capitol, 2005.

CHAPTER 1: YOU CAME OUT OF MY HEAD

1. C. S. Lewis, *The Magician's Nephew* (New York: Macmillan, 1955),
95.

CHAPTER 2: MEET THE ARTIST

1. Viktor E. Frankl, *Man's Search for Meaning* (Boston: Beacon,
2006).
2. The Westminster Shorter Catechism can be accessed at www
.reformed.org/documents/WSC.html.
3. Frankl, *Man's Search*, 116.
4. C. S. Lewis, *The Last Battle* (New York: Macmillan, 1956), 86.

CHAPTER 3: THE COST

1. In this section, I'm relying heavily on Leon Morris's discussion of redemption in *The Apostolic Preaching of the Cross*, 3rd ed. (London: Tyndale, 1965).

2. Tim Keller, "How Can I Know God?," Redeemer Presbyterian Church, June 1991, www.redeemer.com/learn/skeptics_welcome/how _can_i_know_god/.

3. Morris, *Apostolic Preaching*, 29.

4. A phrase taken from Michael J. Behe's *Darwin's Black Box: The Biochemical Challenge to Evolution* (New York: Free Press, 2006), 39ff.

5. This concept was adopted from Tim Keller's *The Reason for God: Belief in an Age of Skepticism* (New York: Dutton, 2008), 192.

6. D. Martyn Lloyd-Jones, *Spiritual Depression: Its Causes and Its Cure* (Grand Rapids, MI: Eerdmans, 1965), 93.

7. Thomas Goodwin, *Of Christ the Mediator*, in *The Works of Thomas Goodwin* (Grand Rapids, MI: Reformation Heritage Books, 2006), 5:7.

8. Goodwin, *Of Christ*, 5:28.

CHAPTER 4: YOUR APPOINTMENT

1. J. Alec Motyer, *The Prophecy of Isaiah: An Introduction and Commentary* (Downers Grove, IL: InterVarsity, 1993).

2. These passages in Isaiah refer to the Savior as: King (9:1–7; 11:1–16; 32:1–8; 33:17–24); Servant (42:1–4; 49:1–6; 50:4–9; 52:13–53:12); Conqueror (59:20–21; 61:1–3; 61:10–62:7; 63:1–6).

3. Romans 16:26 calls it "the obedience of faith."

4. John Bunyan, *Dangerous Journey: The Story of Pilgrim's Progress*, abridged by Oliver Hunkin (Grand Rapids, MI: Eerdmans, 1985), 89–97.

CHAPTER 5: IT WON'T BE TOO MUCH FOR YOU TO HANDLE

1. *What about Bob?*, directed by Frank Oz (Burbank, CA: Touchstone, 1991).

2. *The Notebook*, directed by Nick Cassavetes (New York: New Line, 2004).

3. Prayer can't take the place of Bible reading, but it is often the first step in our relationship with God. Prayer also needs to be a part of our ongoing relationship with God as we read Scripture.

4. Charles H. Spurgeon, *The Treasury of David* (Grand Rapids, MI: Kregel, 1976), 110.

5. Doug Stanton, *Horse Soldiers: The Extraordinary Story of a Band of U.S. Soldiers Who Rode to Victory in Afghanistan* (New York: Scribner, 2009).

CHAPTER 6: THE OLD HEART AND ARROW

1. Ernest Becker, *The Denial of Death* (New York: Simon and Schuster, 1973).

2. Percy Bysshe Shelley, *Shelley: Poems* (New York: Alfred A. Knopf, 1993), 9.

3. John Calvin, *Institutes of the Christian Religion*, trans. Henry Beveridge (Grand Rapids, MI: Eerdmans, 1989), 37.

CHAPTER 7: CHOOSING JUST THE RIGHT ONE

1. It's important to keep in mind that this is a metaphor. God doesn't really have tattoos, since God doesn't really have hands. God is spirit. However, God accommodates to our understanding by using physical imagery.

2. Psalm 121:4 says, "Behold, he who keeps Israel will neither slumber nor sleep."

3. Nigel Turner, *Christian Words* (Edinburgh: T&T Clark, 1980), 262.

4. Jonathan Edwards, *The Works of Jonathan Edwards*, vol. 2 (Carlisle, PA: Banner of Truth Trust, 1974), 869.

5. *Life of Pi*, directed by Ang Lee (Century City, CA: Fox, 2012).

6. *George Herbert: The Complete English Works*, ed. Ann Pasternak Slater (New York: Alfred A. Knopf, 1995), 25.

7. *George Herbert*, xxxi.

8. Shel Silverstein, "A Boy Named Sue," Famous Poets and Poems, accessed July 17, 2014, http://famouspoetsandpoems.com/poets/shel_silverstein/poems/14827.

CHAPTER 8: HOW IT LOOKS IN THE MIRROR

1. Colin Smith told the following story in a sermon titled "The Decision That Really Matters," which he delivered on September 22, 2013, to the Orchard Church in Arlington Heights, Illinois. This can be accessed at http://theorchardefc.org/home/sermons-resources/sermons/view-sermon/?sermon_id=6381.

2. Smith, "Decision," http://theorchardefc.org/home/sermons-resources/sermons/view-sermon/?sermon_id=6381.

3. Søren Kierkegaard, *The Sickness unto Death: A Christian Psychological Exposition for Upbuilding and Awakening*, ed. and trans. Howard V. Hong and Edna H. Hong (Princeton, NJ: Princeton University Press, 1980).

4. I believe that those with Down syndrome, or any other similar syndrome, are just how God wanted them to be. They have much to offer the world, with positive qualities that aren't found in most others. Parents will be the first to recognize the perfection of their child, regardless of what the world calls normal.

5. Her story is found in all four gospels: Matthew, Mark, Luke, and John.

6. "'What Is Love?' Tops Most Searched Google Queries of 2012," ITV, accessed July 18, 2014, www.itv.com/news/2012-12-11/web -users-search-for-meaning-of-love-online-in-2012/.

CHAPTER 9: IT WILL BE HARD TO HIDE

1. Tim Keller, "Puritan Resources for Biblical Counseling," CCEF, accessed July 18, 2014, www.ccef.org/puritan-resources -biblical-counseling.

2. Elie Wiesel, *Night* (New York: Bantam, 1960), 90.

3. *E.T., the Extra-Terrestrial*, directed by Steven Spielberg (Universal City, CA: Universal, 1982).

CHAPTER 10: YOU WILL NEVER BE THE SAME

1. Rudolf Otto, *The Idea of the Holy*, 2nd ed., trans. John W. Harvey (Oxford: Oxford University Press, 1958), 5.

2. Otto, *Idea of the Holy*, 28.

3. This idea was stimulated by a sermon from Colin Smith, "Blessed Are the Poor in Spirit," The Orchard Church, September 2012, www.unlockingthebible.org/blessed-are-the-poor-in-spirit/.

4. Otto, *Idea of the Holy*, 31.

5. George Herbert Palmer, ed., *The English Works of George Herbert*, vol. 3 (Boston: Houghton Mifflin, 1915), 295 (adjusted for modern wording).

6. See Romans 10:14–16, which connects preaching the good news of Jesus with the responsiveness of the human heart, according to Isaiah 53:1.

7. David W. Pao, *Acts and the Isaianic New Exodus* (Grand Rapids, MI: Baker Academic, 2002), 91–96.

8. In the original Greek, the English phrase "without hindrance" is just one word.

CHAPTER 11: THE NAME ON YOUR ARM

1. This idea for the Spirit's work came from Douglas A. Campbell, "The Story of Jesus in Romans and Galatians," in *Narrative Dynamics in Paul: A Critical Assessment*, ed. Bruce W. Longenecker (Louisville, KY: Westminster John Knox, 2002), 97–124. The "story behind the story" concept also came from Campbell's chapter, where he discussed a "narrative reading of Paul."

AFTER CARE

1. For instance, start reading 1 Peter, from chapter 1 to chapter 5.